Common CORE Writing to Texts

C0-AVE-829

Table of Contents

Introduction

What Is the Common Core?

The Common Core State Standards are an initiative by states to set shared, consistent, and clear expectations of what students are expected to learn. This helps teachers and parents know what they need to do to help students. The standards are designed to be rigorous and pertinent to the real world. They reflect the knowledge and skills that young people need for success in college and careers.

If your state has joined the Common Core State Standards Initiative, then teachers are required to incorporate these standards into their lesson plans. Students need targeted practice in order to meet grade-level standards and expectations, and thereby be promoted to the next grade.

What Does It Mean to Write to Texts?

One of the most important instructional shifts in the Common Core State Standards is writing to texts, or sources. What exactly does this mean? Haven't standardized assessments always used reading texts as a springboard to writing? Yes, but the required writing hasn't always been DEPENDENT on the key ideas and details in a text.

A prompt that is non-text-dependent asks students to rely on prior knowledge or experience. In fact, students could likely carry out the writing without reading the text at all. The writing does not need to include ideas, information, and key vocabulary from the text.

Writing to texts requires students to analyze, clarify, and cite information they read in the text. The writing reveals whether students have performed a close reading, because it is designed to elicit ideas, information, and key vocabulary from the text as well as students' own evidence-based inferences and conclusions. These are all skills that prepare them for the grades ahead, college, the workplace, and real-world applications in their adult daily lives.

An example of a passage with non-text-dependent and text-dependent sample prompts is provided on page 3.

Common Core Writing to Texts Grade 5 • ©2014 Newmark Learning, LLC

Sample Passage

Simple and Compound Machines

1.   A simple machine is a tool that does work with one movement. Like all machines, a simple machine makes work easier. It has few or no moving parts and uses energy to do work. A lever, a wedge, a screw, a pulley, a wheel and axle, and an inclined plane are all simple machines.

2.   You use simple machines all the time, too. If you have ever played on a seesaw or walked up a ramp, then you have used a simple machine. If you have opened a door, eaten with a spoon, cut with scissors, or zipped up a zipper, you have used a simple machine.

3.   A compound machine is made of two or more simple machines. For example, the pedals, wheels, and gears on a bicycle are wheels and axles, and the hand brakes on the handlebars are levers. Cars, airplanes, watches, and washing machines are also examples of compound machines. Compound machines are very useful because they can do the work of many simple machines at the same time.

4.   Life would be very different if we did not have machines. Work would be much harder, and playing wouldn't be as much fun.

Standard	Sample Prompt: Non-Text-Dependent	Sample Prompt: Text-Dependent
W.5.1 (Opinion/ Argument)	Do you prefer zippers, buttons, buckles, or another type of fastener for your clothing? Why?	The author makes three claims in the last paragraph. Choose one of the claims, tell whether you agree or disagree, and support your opinion with evidence from the text.
W.5.2 (Informative/ Explanatory)	Think about a machine you have used to do a task. How did you use it? How did using the machine make the task easier?	Compare and contrast simple and compound machines. Use details from the text to support your explanation.
W.5.3 (Narrative)	Write a story in which a character invents a machine that no one has seen or heard of before.	Imagine that all the machines mentioned in the passage disappeared for twenty-four hours. Write a journal entry about how your life was different that day and what you learned.

Using This Book

How Does This Book Help Students?

This book is organized into four main sections: Writing Mini-Lessons, Practice Texts with Prompts, Graphic Organizers and Checklists, and Rubrics and Assessments. All mini-lessons and practice pages are self-contained and may be used in any order that meets the needs of students. The elements of this book work together to provide students with the tools they need to be able to master the range of skills and application as required by the Common Core.

1. Mini-Lessons for Opinion/Argument, Informative/Explanatory, and Narrative Writing

Writing mini-lessons prepares students to use writing as a way to state and support opinions, demonstrate understanding of the subjects they are studying, and convey real and imagined experiences. The mini-lessons are organized in the order of the standards, but you may wish to do them with your class in an order that matches your curriculum. For each type of writing the first mini-lesson covers responding to one text, while the second mini-lesson models how to respond to multiple texts.

Each mini-lesson begins with a lesson plan that provides step-by-step instruction.

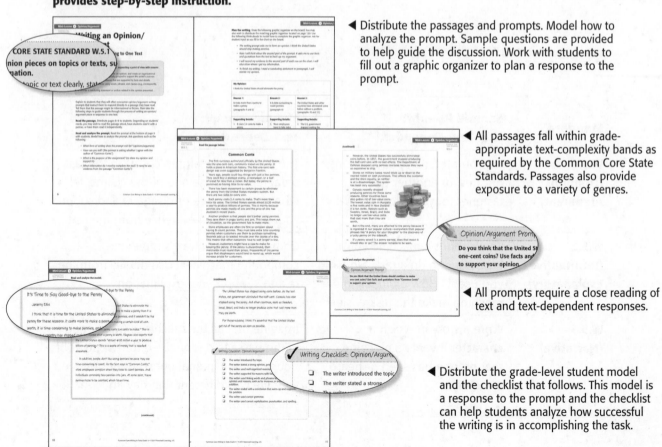

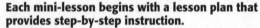

◀ Distribute the passages and prompts. Model how to analyze the prompt. Sample questions are provided to help guide the discussion. Work with students to fill out a graphic organizer to plan a response to the prompt.

◀ All passages fall within grade-appropriate text-complexity bands as required by the Common Core State Standards. Passages also provide exposure to a variety of genres.

◀ All prompts require a close reading of text and text-dependent responses.

◀ Distribute the grade-level student model and the checklist that follows. This model is a response to the prompt and the checklist can help students analyze how successful the writing is in accomplishing the task.

2. Practice Texts with Prompts

Passages and prompts provide students with real experience writing to a single text and multiple texts. The first ten lessons require students to respond to one text. The last ten require students to respond to multiple texts.

Each passage or pair of passages is followed by three text-dependent prompts: Opinion/Argument, Informative/Explanatory, and Narrative. You may wish to assign a particular prompt, have students choose one, or have them execute each type of writing over a longer period of time.

For more information on how to use this section, see page 48.

3. Graphic Organizers and Checklists

For each type of writing, you can distribute a corresponding graphic organizer and checklist to help students plan and evaluate their writing.

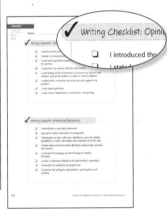

4. Rubrics and Assessments

The section includes Evaluation Rubrics to guide your assessment and scoring of students' responses. Based on your observations of students' writing, use the differentiated rubrics. These are designed to help you conduct meaningful conferences with students and will help differentiate your interactions to match students' needs.

For each score a student receives in the Evaluation Rubrics, responsive prompts are provided. These gradual-release prompts scaffold writers toward mastery of each writing type.

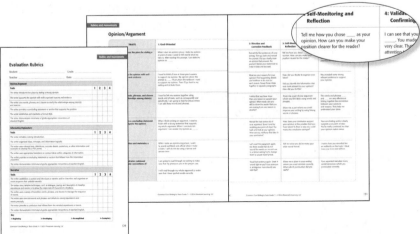

COMMON CORE
STATE STANDARD
W.5.1

Writing an Opinion/Argument

Mini-Lesson 1: **Writing to One Text**

> **COMMON CORE STATE STANDARD W.5.1**
>
> **Write opinion pieces on topics or texts, supporting a point of view with reasons and information.**
>
> a. Introduce a topic or text clearly, state an opinion, and create an organizational structure in which ideas are logically grouped to support the writer's purpose.
>
> b. Provide logically ordered reasons that are supported by facts and details.
>
> c. Link opinion and reasons using words, phrases, and clauses (e.g., *consequently, specifically*).
>
> d. Provide a concluding statement or section related to the opinion presented.

Explain to students that they will often encounter opinion/argument writing prompts that instruct them to respond directly to a passage they have read. Tell them that the passage might be informational or fiction. Then take the following steps to guide students through the process of writing an opinion/argument piece in response to one text.

Read the passage. Distribute pages 8–9 to students. Depending on students' needs, you may wish to read the passage aloud, have students read it with a partner, or have them read it independently.

Read and analyze the prompt. Read the prompt at the bottom of page 9 with students. Model how to analyze the prompt. Ask questions such as the following:

- *What form of writing does the prompt ask for?* (opinion/argument)

- *How can you tell?* (The prompt is asking whether I agree with the author of "Common Cents.")

- *What is the purpose of the assignment?* (to state my opinion and support it)

- *What information do I need to complete the task?* (I need to use evidence from the passage "Common Cents.")

Plan the writing. Draw the following graphic organizer on the board. You may also wish to distribute the matching graphic organizer located on page 120. Use the following think-alouds to model how to complete the graphic organizer. Ask for student input as you fill in the chart on the board.

- *The writing prompt asks me to form an opinion. I think the United States should stop making pennies.*

- *Now I will think about the second part of the prompt. It asks me to use facts and quotations from the text to back up my argument.*

- *I will record my evidence in the second part of each row on the chart. I will also show where I got my information.*

- *To finish my writing, I need a concluding statement or paragraph. I will restate my opinion.*

My Opinion:

I think the United States should eliminate the penny.

Reason 1:	**Reason 2:**	**Reason 3:**
It costs more than a penny to make a penny. (paragraphs 4 and 5)	It is time-consuming to count pennies. (paragraph 6)	The United States and other countries have eliminated coins before without a problem. (paragraphs 10 and 12)
Supporting Details: 1. It costs 2.4 cents to make a penny. 2. The United States spends $120 million a year to make pennies. 3. People take pennies out of circulation, so the government has to make more.	**Supporting Details:** 1. Store employees have to take extra time to count pennies. 2. Individuals spend time counting pennies, too.	**Supporting Details:** 1. The U.S. government stopped making the half-cent. 2. Canada stopped making pennies. 3. Other nations no longer make coins that cost more than they're worth.

My Opinion Restated:

I think the United States should get rid of the penny.

Read and analyze the model. Distribute the student writing model and checklist on pages 10–11 to students. Read them aloud. Discuss with students whether or not the writer was successful at accomplishing the task. Ask them to complete the checklist as you discuss the opinion/argument piece.

COMMON CORE
STATE STANDARD

W.5.1

Read the passage below.

Common Cents

1. The first currency authorized officially by the United States was the one-cent coin, commonly known as the penny. It holds a place in American history. The first one-cent coin design was even suggested by Benjamin Franklin.

2. Years ago, people could buy things with just a few pennies. They could buy a postage stamp, a newspaper, or a loaf of bread for less than a nickel. But today, the penny is perceived as having little to no value.

3. There has been movement by certain groups to eliminate the penny from the United States monetary system. But there are two sides to every coin.

4. Each penny costs 2.4 cents to make. That's more than twice its value. The United States spends almost $120 million a year to produce billions of pennies. This is mainly because pennies are made mostly of zinc and the price of zinc has doubled in recent years.

5. Another problem is that people don't bother using pennies. They save them in piggy banks and jars. This keeps them out of circulation, so the government has to make more.

6. Store employees are often the first to complain about having to count pennies. They must take extra time counting pennies when customers use them to purchase something. Seconds add up to wasted minutes over the course of a day. This means that other customers have to wait longer in line.

7. However, customers might have a case to make for keeping the penny. If the penny is discontinued, then merchants must round their prices. Proponents of the penny argue that shopkeepers would tend to round up, which would increase prices for customers.

8. Many charity organizations also rely on pennies for money. Pennies can add up quickly, and organizations can total donations in the thousands just from spare change alone.

9. People seeking to abolish the penny can look to other countries for examples of where the relative equivalent of the one-cent coin is still in production. When the European Union decided to switch to euros, it kept the one-euro cent in production to avoid the rounding up of prices.

(continued)

(continued)

10.   However, the United States has successfully eliminated coins before. In 1857, the government stopped producing the half-cent coin with no bad effects. The Department of Defense stopped using pennies overseas because they were so expensive to ship.

11.   Stores on military bases round totals up or down to the nearest nickel on cash purchases. That affects the customer and the store equally, so neither is at a disadvantage. The system has been very successful.

12.   Canada recently stopped producing pennies for these same reasons. Other countries have also gotten rid of low-value coins. The lowest value coin in Australia is five cents and in New Zealand it is ten cents. Nations such as Sweden, Israel, Brazil, and India no longer use low-value coins that cost more than they are worth.

13.   But in the end, many are attached to the penny because it is ingrained in our popular culture—everywhere from popular phrases like "A penny for your thoughts" to the discovery of a lucky penny on the sidewalk.

14.   If a penny saved is a penny earned, does that mean it should stay or go? The answer remains to be seen.

Read and analyze the prompt.

Opinion/Argument Prompt

Do you think that the United States should continue to make one-cent coins? Use facts and quotations from "Common Cents" to support your opinion.

Read and analyze the model.

It's Time to Say Good-bye to the Penny

Jeremy Ellis

I think that it is time for the United States to eliminate the penny for these reasons: it costs more to make a penny than it is worth, it is time-consuming to make pennies, and it wouldn't be the first time a country has stopped making a certain kind of coin.

The text says, "each penny costs 2.4 cents to make." This is more than double what a penny is worth. Hughes also reports that the United States spends "almost $120 million a year to produce billions of pennies." This is a waste of money that is needed elsewhere.

In addition, people don't like using pennies because they are time-consuming to count. As the text says in "Common Cents," store employees complain when they have to count pennies. And individuals commonly toss pennies into jars. At some point, these pennies have to be counted, which takes time.

(continued)

(continued)

The United States has stopped using coins before. As the text states, our government eliminated the half-cent. Canada has also stopped using the penny. And other countries, such as Sweden, Israel, Brazil, and India no longer produce coins that cost more than they are worth.

For these reasons, I think it's essential that the United States get rid of the penny as soon as possible.

✔ Writing Checklist: Opinion/Argument

- ❏ The writer introduced the topic.
- ❏ The writer stated a strong opinion, position, or point of view.
- ❏ The writer used well-organized reasons to support his opinion.
- ❏ The writer supported his reasons with facts and details.
- ❏ The writer used linking words and phrases to connect his opinion and reasons, such as *for instance*, *in order to*, and *in addition*.
- ❏ The writer ended with a conclusion that sums up and supports his position.
- ❏ The writer used correct grammar.
- ❏ The writer used correct capitalization, punctuation, and spelling.

COMMON CORE
STATE STANDARD
W.5.1

Writing an Opinion/ Argument

Mini-Lesson 2: **Writing to Multiple Texts**

COMMON CORE STATE STANDARD W.5.1

Write opinion pieces on topics or texts, supporting a point of view with reasons and information.

a. Introduce a topic or text clearly, state an opinion, and create an organizational structure in which ideas are logically grouped to support the writer's purpose.

b. Provide logically ordered reasons that are supported by facts and details.

c. Link opinion and reasons using words, phrases, and clauses (e.g., *consequently, specifically*).

d. Provide a concluding statement or section related to the opinion presented.

Explain to students that they will often encounter writing prompts that instruct them to respond directly to more than one passage. For example, they might have to read two informational passages about the same topic or two fiction passages by the same author. Then take the following steps to guide students through the process of writing an opinion/argument in response to multiple texts.

Read the passages. Distribute pages 14–17 to students. Depending on students' needs, you may wish to read the passages aloud, have students read them with a partner, or have them read the passages independently.

Read and analyze the prompt. Read the prompt at the bottom of page 17 with students. Model how to analyze the prompt. Ask questions such as the following:

- *What form of writing does the prompt ask for?* (opinion/argument)

- *How can you tell?* (The prompt is asking which letter I agree with more and why.)

- *What is the purpose of the assignment?* (to state my opinion and support it with evidence)

- *What information do I need to complete the task?* (I need to use evidence from both "Year-Round Schooling Is the Way to Go" and "Say No to Year-Round Schooling.")

Plan the writing. Draw the following graphic organizer on the board. You may also wish to distribute the matching graphic organizer located on page 121. Use the following think-alouds to model how to complete the graphic organizer. Ask for student input as you fill in the chart on the board.

- *The writing prompt asks me to form an opinion about which letter I agree with more. I agree more with "Year-Round Schooling Is the Way to Go" because it seems as if having shorter breaks throughout the year is better for students than having one long summer break.*

- *Now I will think about the second part of the prompt. It asks me to support my opinion with reasons from the letters and my own ideas.*

- *I will record my reasons and my evidence in the chart.*

- *To finish my writing, I need a concluding statement or paragraph. I will restate my opinion by explaining why I agree more with the author of the first letter.*

Introduction		
Position Sentence: I agree more with the author of "Year-Round Schooling Is the Way to Go."		
Reason 1: It is better for children's education.	**Reason 2**: Year-round schooling will help working parents.	**Reason 3:** Children no longer need such a long break.
Reason 1 Evidence: Kids forget what they have learned over the summer. Teachers have to reteach material that students have forgotten. Because of this, other countries no longer have such a long summer break.	**Reason 2 Evidence:** Parents often struggle to find child care during the summer. It is better for kids to continue their daily schedule year-round.	**Reason 3 Evidence:** Our country has such a long summer break because kids were once needed to help on the farm. This is no longer the case.
My Conclusion: Restate position: I think it's time to switch to year-round schooling because it's better for children.		

Read and analyze the model. Distribute the student writing model and checklist on pages 18–19 to students. Read them aloud. Discuss with students whether or not the writer was successful at accomplishing the task. Ask them to complete the checklist as you discuss the opinion/argument piece.

COMMON CORE
STATE STANDARD
W.5.1

Read the passages.

Year-Round Schooling Is the Way to Go

1. Dear Editor,

2.   Some people object to the idea of year-round schooling for children. However, there are many good reasons why we should do away with long summer breaks.

3.   Children forget a great deal when they're away from the classroom. Before they can begin new lessons in the fall, teachers must review the material that was covered the year before. This wastes too much classroom time.

4.   Having only a short break in the summer makes it less likely that children will forget what they have learned. Other countries do not have such a long summer break for this reason. Few countries offer more than seven consecutive weeks of vacation. The United States is the only country that offers, on average, thirteen weeks.

5.   Children who are struggling in school would no longer have to go to summer school. Students who need extra help would be able to get it throughout the year. This would save school districts money because they would not have to include summer school in their annual budgets.

6.   Some parents are afraid that they won't be able to go on family vacations if the school year is extended. However, with year-round education, vacation is more evenly distributed throughout the year. Under most plans, students are offered breaks of two or three weeks at a time. Families are not limited to traveling only in the summer. Many enjoy a winter vacation in a warm place.

7.   Year-round school would be an enormous benefit for working parents in terms of child care. They wouldn't have to make special arrangements for the summer months or spend extra money. Their children would feel more comfortable, too, if they could continue their daily schedule year-round.

(continued)

(continued)

8.   Long summer breaks were needed years ago when we were a farm-based society. Back then, children were needed to plant and harvest crops. However, our society no longer depends on child labor. It is now better for our children to focus on their education throughout the year.

9.   We need to work together and do what's best for our children. It's time to extend the school year.

10. Amy McDonald

(continue to next passage)

(continued)

Say No to Year-Round Schooling

1. Dear Editor,

2.   Not everyone agrees that more time in school is better for children. The quality of education that children receive is more important than the amount of time they spend in a classroom. Some studies have found little or no connection between success in school and the length of the school year. How children spend their time in the classroom is much more important than the number of hours they sit at a desk. Children must be engaged in the learning process. This is what leads to academic success.

3.   Year-round schooling would be especially troublesome for children who find it difficult to pay attention for long periods of time. This is true of children with attention-deficit hyperactivity disorder (ADHD). It is also true of young children, who need to spend a long period of time each year playing outdoors in warm weather. Year-round schooling would only lead to behavioral problems in the classroom.

4.   Making students attend school during the summer will make it hard for students who rely on full-time work during these months. Many teens in our school district work full time during the summer. They save their earnings for college. They will not be able to do this if they are forced to go to school all year. Some may not have enough money to attend college because of this.

5.   Year-round schooling will cost school districts too much money. Costs for supplies, buses, salaries, and heating and air-conditioning are rising every year. Most schools have to cut costs wherever they can. Keeping schools open for nine months is expensive. Providing services all year would only increase this financial strain and would lead to higher school taxes for the citizens in our school district.

(continued)

(continued)

6.   Lastly, children need time off during the summer to enjoy life experiences. They need time to spend with their family, travel, participate in sports, go to summer camp, or participate in activities that are not related to school. They should be given time to meet new people of different ages and backgrounds.

7.   Let's concentrate on the quality of our schools and let kids be kids during the summer.

8.   Nick Castellino

Read and analyze the prompt.

Writing Prompt

Based on the opinions and details in these two letters, which letter do you agree with more and why? Support your opinion with details from both of the letters.

Read and analyze the model.

Children Would Benefit from Year-Round Schooling

by Paul Sanders

After carefully reading "Year-Round Schooling Is the Way to Go," by Amy McDonald, and "Say No to Year-Round Schooling," by Nick Castellino, I am convinced that year-round schooling is better for children. The evidence is clear that it is better for children's education. It will help working parents, and children no longer need such a long break.

As McDonald explains, children forget what they have learned over the summer. Teachers have to reteach material, which wastes time. If kids had short breaks throughout the year, this would not happen. As McDonald explains, other countries no longer have such long breaks for this reason.

Nick Castellino stated that "Year-round schooling will cost school districts too much money." However, it costs parents more money not to have it. With such a long summer break, parents often have to make special child-care arrangements in the summer.

(continued)

(continued)

Lastly, Castellino stated that we should "let kids be kids during the summer." However, I think McDonald's case is more convincing. She stated that long summer breaks are no longer needed. Summer break was originally intended to allow children to help their families plant and harvest crops. We are no longer a farm-based society. Our children are no longer needed at home in the summer.

For these reasons, I think Amy McDonald's letter is more convincing.

✔ Writing Checklist: Opinion/Argument

❑ The writer introduced the topic.

❑ The writer stated a strong opinion, position, or point of view.

❑ The writer used well-organized reasons from both passages to support his opinion.

❑ The writer supported his reasons with facts and details.

❑ The writer used linking words and phrases to connect his opinion and reasons, such as *for instance*, *in order to*, and *in addition*.

❑ The writer ended with a conclusion that sums up and supports his position.

❑ The writer used correct grammar.

❑ The writer used correct capitalization, punctuation, and spelling.

COMMON CORE
STATE STANDARD
W.5.2

Writing an Informative/ Explanatory Text

Mini-Lesson 3: Writing to One Text

COMMON CORE STATE STANDARD W.5.2

Write informative/explanatory texts to examine a topic and convey ideas and information clearly.

a. Introduce a topic clearly, provide a general observation and focus, and group related information logically; include formatting (e.g., headings), illustrations, and multimedia when useful to aiding comprehension.

b. Develop the topic with facts, definitions, concrete details, quotations, or other information and examples related to the topic.

c. Link ideas within and across categories of information using words, phrases, and clauses (e.g., *in contrast, especially*).

d. Use precise language and domain-specific vocabulary to inform about or explain the topic.

e. Provide a concluding statement or section related to the information or explanation presented.

Explain to students that they will often encounter informative/explanatory writing prompts that instruct them to respond directly to a passage they have read. Tell them that the passage might be nonfiction or fiction. Then take the following steps to guide students through the process of informative/ explanatory writing in response to one text.

Read the passage. Distribute pages 22–23 to students. Depending on students' needs, you may wish to read the passage aloud, have students read it with a partner, or have them read it independently.

Read and analyze the prompt. Read the prompt at the bottom of page 23 with students. Model how to analyze the prompt. Ask questions such as the following:

- *What form of writing does the prompt ask for?* (informative/ explanatory)

- *How can you tell?* (The prompt is asking me to explain why a statement the author made is true using facts from the article.)

- *What is the purpose of the assignment?* (to explain a topic and give information about it)

- *What information do I need to complete the task?* (I need to use evidence from the passage "Stink Bugs.")

Plan the writing. Draw the following graphic organizer on the board. You may also wish to distribute the matching graphic organizer located on page 122. Use the following think-alouds to model how to complete the graphic organizer. Ask for student input as you fill in the chart on the board.

- *The writing prompt asks me to explain why stink bugs are considered pests. Next the prompt asks me to use other facts from the text to explain why this is true.*

- *I will record my evidence in the chart.*

- *To finish my writing, I need a concluding statement or paragraph.*

Topic: Stink bugs

Main Idea:

The author says that stink bugs are considered pests.

Evidence/Details:

1. Stink bugs reproduce quickly.

2. They can harm and even destroy crops.

3. They can live in houses and infest them.

Read and analyze the model. Distribute the student writing model and checklist on pages 24–25 to students. Read them aloud. Discuss with students whether or not the writer was successful at accomplishing this task. Ask them to complete the checklist as you discuss the informative/explanatory text.

COMMON CORE
STATE STANDARD
W.5.2

Read the passage below.

Stink Bugs

1.   Stink bugs are a type of bug that is native to East Asia but was accidentally introduced to the United States in the late 1990s. Stink bugs quickly established themselves in large populations. They are difficult to manage because of their large number and large range.

Description

2.   Many types of stink bugs exist, so the size of individuals varies. Most adult stink bugs are from 8 to 10 millimeters (0.3 to 0.4 inch) in length. Adults have four wings, six legs, and two antennae. Their beaks are long and narrow. Stink bugs are usually green or brown. Some also have bright white markings. Stink bugs are easy to recognize because they look like they are wearing a triangular shield of armor on their back. Despite their name, stink bugs do not actually stink—unless they are crushed. Then they release a bad smell.

Behavior

3.   Most adult stink bugs are active between May and October. In cooler climates, adults hibernate, or sleep, during the winter. In warmer climates, stink bugs don't hibernate but are much less active during the winter.

4.   Female stink bugs lay large groups of eggs. The eggs are shaped like barrels, which they place in rows. Females stay close to their eggs to guard them and the larva when they hatch.

Diet

5.   Most adult stink bugs are herbivores, which means they feed on plant life, such as leaves, flowers, fruit, and crops. Some types of stink bugs are omnivores. They eat other insects, including caterpillars, as well as plants and crops.

(continued)

(continued)

Habitat

6. Stink bugs thrive in many different habitats. Outdoors they live in crop fields, orchards, and gardens. However, they also live quite comfortably indoors. Stink bugs can enter houses in many ways, but their nests are most commonly found in attics. They reproduce quickly and can infest a home.

Impact

7. Stink bugs are not harmful to people but are considered pests. This is mostly because they appear in large numbers and reproduce quickly. Stink bugs can be harmful to plant life. They can scar the plants or crops they feed on. If they are present in large numbers, stink bugs can cause crops to fail.

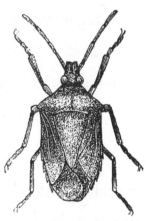

Read and analyze the prompt.

Informative/Explanatory Prompt

In paragraph 7, the text states, "Stink bugs are not harmful to people but are considered pests." Use facts from the text to explain why this is true.

COMMON CORE
STATE STANDARD
W.5.2

Read and analyze the model.

Why Stink Bugs Are Pests

Breanne Romano

The author of "Stink Bugs" says that "Stink bugs are not harmful to people but are considered pests." Stink bugs are considered pests mainly because they reproduce quickly, they harm crops, and they infest homes.

First, stink bugs are pests because they reproduce quickly. Since they were accidentally introduced to the United States in the late 1990s, stink bug populations have grown rapidly. In paragraph 1, the text states that stink bugs are "difficult to manage because of their large number and large range." In paragraph 7, the article says that they "appear in large numbers and reproduce quickly."

In addition, the author says that stink bugs can thrive in many different habitats and can be harmful to plant life. They can scar the plants they feed on and if they are present in large numbers, they can cause crops to fail.

Finally, stink bugs can also live comfortably in homes and can infest a home. They can easily enters homes and often make nests in the attics of people's homes.

In summary, stink bugs are pests because their population grows rapidly, they are a danger to plant life, and they make nests in people's homes.

COMMON CORE
STATE STANDARD
W.5.2

✔ Writing Checklist: Informative/Explanatory

❏ The writer started with a clear topic statement.

❏ The writer grouped related information in paragraphs.

❏ The writer developed her topic with facts, definitions, concrete details, quotations, or other information and examples from the text.

❏ The writer linked ideas and information effectively using words, phrases, and clauses.

❏ The writer used precise language and terminology to explain the topic.

❏ The writer wrote a conclusion related to the information presented.

❏ The writer reviewed her writing for good grammar.

❏ The writer reviewed her writing for capitalization, punctuation, and spelling.

COMMON CORE
STATE STANDARD
W.5.2

Writing an Informative/ Explanatory Text

Mini-Lesson 4: Writing to Multiple Texts

COMMON CORE STATE STANDARD W.5.2

Write informative/explanatory texts to examine a topic and convey ideas and information clearly.

a. Introduce a topic clearly, provide a general observation and focus, and group related information logically; include formatting (e.g., headings), illustrations, and multimedia when useful to aiding comprehension.

b. Develop the topic with facts, definitions, concrete details, quotations, or other information and examples related to the topic.

c. Link ideas within and across categories of information using words, phrases, and clauses (e.g., *in contrast*, *especially*).

d. Use precise language and domain-specific vocabulary to inform about or explain the topic.

e. Provide a concluding statement or section related to the information or explanation presented.

Explain to students that they will often encounter writing prompts that instruct them to respond directly to more than one passage. For example, they might have to read two informational passages about the same topic or two fiction passages by the same author. Then take the following steps to guide students through the process of writing an informative/explanatory piece in response to multiple texts.

Read the passages. Distribute pages 28–31 to students. Depending on students' needs, you may wish to read the passages aloud, have students read them with a partner, or have them read the passages independently.

Read and analyze the prompt. Read the prompt at the bottom of page 31 with students. Model how to analyze the prompt. Ask questions such as the following:

- *What form of writing does the prompt ask for?* (informative/ explanatory)

- *How can you tell?* (The prompt is asking me to explain something and provide information.)

- *What is the purpose of the assignment?* (to explain a topic and give information about it)

- *What information do I need to complete the task?* (I need to use evidence from the passage "Life in Australia" and the passage "Facts about Australia.")

COMMON CORE
STATE STANDARD
W.5.2

Plan the writing. Draw the following graphic organizer on the board. You may also wish to distribute the matching graphic organizer located on page 123. Use the following think-alouds to model how to complete the graphic organizer. Ask for student input as you fill in the chart on the board.

- *The writing prompt asks me to use information from both passages to explain why someone from another country might want to move to Australia.*

- *I will record my evidence in the chart.*

- *To finish my writing, I need a concluding statement or paragraph.*

Topic:
Why someone from another country might want to move to Australia

Main Point:	**Supporting Details:**
Australia has interesting wildlife. People can see animals there that do not live anywhere else in the world.	They can see animals like the platypus, the kangaroo, and the koala. They can see birds like the kookaburra and the emu.
Main Point:	**Supporting Details:**
Australia has an excellent, flexible educational system.	Students who live very far from a school can attend a "school of the air." They can attend school via the Internet.
Main Point:	**Supporting Details:**
Australia is one of the wealthiest countries in the world.	The country offers economic freedom and people enjoy excellent health-care services.

Read and analyze the model. Distribute the student writing model and checklist on pages 32–33 to students. Read them aloud. Discuss with students whether or not the writer was successful at accomplishing this task. Ask them to complete the checklist as you discuss the informative/explanatory text.

Read the passages.

Life in Australia

1.   The Commonwealth of Australia is an unusual island that's so big that it is also a continent. It's sometimes called "Down Under" because of its location below the equator.

2.   One of the most interesting things about Australia is its wildlife. It has amazing animals that live nowhere else in the world.

3.   The platypus, the kangaroo, and the koala evolved on the island and are unlike creatures in other parts of the world. They are marsupials that carry their young in a pouch. The babies, called "joeys," are only the size of a jelly bean when they're born. They live in their mother's pouch until they're big enough to go out into the world.

4.   Birds such as the kookaburra, a type of kingfisher that has a strange call that sounds like a person laughing, also live in Australia. The emu is another. It is almost as big as an ostrich and is Australia's largest native bird.

5.   Children in Australia enjoy sports and games. They play soccer, rugby, and cricket. They also play "Aussie Rules Football." It is a very fast, rough game that involves eighteen players on the field. As in American football, players run, kick, tackle, and pass the football. But in Aussie Rules, the object is to kick the football between the goalposts.

6.   Australia's schools, called "stations," may be very large or very small, depending upon whether they are located in cities or near large farms. But some children live too far from a school to attend. For those children, Australia has "schools of the air."

7.   When school starts, students receive a package of materials that includes videos, library books, and computer software. A teacher presents lessons over the Internet and can hear the class members if they ask questions.

(continued)

COMMON CORE
STATE STANDARD

W.5.2

(continued)

8.   Then the students do their work on their own. They study about five hours a day. They can ask an older brother or sister, a parent, or a tutor for help if they need it. Once a year, they go to town for a week and work as a class.

(continue to next passage)

(continued)

Facts About Australia

1. Australia is the sixth-largest country in the world by total area. It includes the island of Tasmania and several smaller islands, as well as the main island/continent. The total area is almost 3 million square miles.

2. One of the wealthiest countries in the world, Australia also offers economic freedom, the protection of civil liberties, and excellent services in health and education.

3. Australia has six states: New South Wales, Queensland, South Australia, Tasmania, Victoria, and Western Australia. It also has two major mainland territories called the Australian Capital Territory and the Northern Territory, which also generally function as states.

4. Australia's climate varies with its geography. There are rain forests, mountain ranges, deserts, and grasslands. The dry land called the "outback" is the largest area. Only the southwestern and southeastern areas of the continent have a temperate climate. Naturally, that's where most people on the island live.

(continued)

COMMON CORE
STATE STANDARD
W.5.2

(continued)

For more information about Australia, see:

 <u>Cities</u>

 <u>Climate</u>

 <u>Culture</u>

 <u>Education</u>

 <u>Environment</u>

 <u>Government</u>

 <u>Health</u>

 <u>History</u>

 <u>Maps</u>

 <u>People</u>

 <u>Sports</u>

 <u>Wildlife</u>

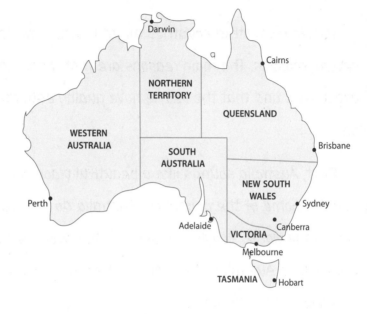

Read and analyze the prompt.

Informative/Explanatory Prompt

Use information from both "Life in Australia" and "Facts About Australia" to explain why someone from another country might want to move to Australia.

COMMON CORE
STATE STANDARD
W.5.2

Read and analyze the model.

The Benefits of Living in Australia

by Francis Ostrowski

People from other countries might like to move to Australia for several reasons. The main reasons are that it has unique wildlife to experience and that the people have quality education and health care.

First, Australia sounds like a beautiful place with incredible wildlife. Some of the animals in Australia do not live anywhere else in the world. People can see the platypus, the kangaroo, and the koala in Australia. They can see beautiful birds such as the kookaburra and the emu.

Furthermore, Australia is a wealthy country, and its children enjoy an excellent, flexible school system. They can attend schools at "stations," but if they live too far away, they can attend "schools of the air." These schools allow children to go to school via the Internet. People in Australia also have excellent health care.

Because Australia is filled with incredible wildlife and provides its people with a good quality of life, people might like to move to the land "Down Under."

✔ Writing Checklist: Informative/Explanatory

- ❏ The writer started with a clear topic statement.

- ❏ The writer grouped related information in paragraphs.

- ❏ The writer developed his topic with facts, definitions, concrete details, quotations, or other information and examples from the text.

- ❏ The writer linked ideas and information effectively using words, phrases, and clauses.

- ❏ The writer used precise language and terminology to explain the topic.

- ❏ The writer wrote a conclusion related to the information he presented.

- ❏ The writer reviewed his writing for good grammar.

- ❏ The writer reviewed his writing for capitalization, punctuation, and spelling.

COMMON CORE
STATE STANDARD
W.5.3

Writing a Narrative
Mini-Lesson 5: **Writing to One Text**

COMMON CORE STATE STANDARD W.5.3

Write narratives to develop real or imagined experiences or events using effective technique, descriptive details, and clear event sequences.

a. Orient the reader by establishing a situation and introducing a narrator and/or characters; organize an event sequence that unfolds naturally.

b. Use narrative techniques, such as dialogue, description, and pacing, to develop experiences and events or show the responses of characters to situations.

c. Use a variety of transitional words, phrases, and clauses to manage the sequence of events.

d. Use concrete words and phrases and sensory details to convey experiences and events precisely.

e. Provide a conclusion that follows from the narrated experiences or events.

Explain to students that they will often encounter narrative writing prompts that instruct them to respond directly to a text they have read. The text may be fiction or informational. Then take the following steps to guide students through the process of writing a narrative piece in response to one text.

Read the passage. Distribute pages 36–37 to students. Depending on students' needs, you may wish to read the passage aloud, have students read it with a partner, or have them read it independently.

Read and analyze the prompt. Read the prompt at the bottom of page 37 with students. Model how to analyze the prompt. Ask questions such as the following:

- *What form of writing does the prompt ask for?* (narrative)

- *How can you tell?* (The prompt asks me to write a story from Dad's point of view.)

- *What is the purpose of the assignment?* (to write a story)

- *What information do I need to complete the task?* (I need to use evidence from the story "Jeremy's Big Catch.")

Plan the writing. Draw the following graphic organizer on the board. You may also wish to distribute the matching graphic organizer located on page 124. Use the following think-alouds to model how to complete the graphic organizer. Ask for student input as you fill in the chart on the board.

- *The writing prompt asks me to rewrite the story "Jeremy's Big Catch" from Dad's point of view.*

- *I need to be sure that I tell what Dad thinks and how he feels.*

- *I need to tell my story using the pronouns **I** and **we**.*

- *I will record my events in the chart.*

Major Events
1. I decided to take my son Jeremy and my niece Kayla fly-fishing.
2. Jeremy loaded our fishing gear into the car, and we picked up Kayla.
3. I explained the basics of fly-fishing as we drove to the river.
4. We all put on our waders, and Jeremy laughed.
5. I told the kids to be careful walking into the river.
6. I taught them how to cast their lines.
7. Jeremy caught a huge trout.
8. Kayla took his picture.
9. We had a great time.

Read and analyze the model. Distribute the student writing model and checklist on pages 38–39 to students. Read them aloud. Discuss with students whether or not the writer was successful at accomplishing the task. Ask them to complete the checklist as you discuss the narrative.

Read the passage below.

Jeremy's Big Catch

1. "Jeremy, did you get the fishing rods from the basement?" Dad asked.

2. "Yes, they're near the front door," Jeremy replied.

3. Dad was taking Jeremy and his cousin Kayla fly-fishing for the first time. They were going to a local lake that was known for its abundance of trout. Dad had fished all his life and had the necessary equipment.

4. Jeremy helped Dad load the car with the fishing gear. There were fishing rods, fishing lines, artificial flies, and other items. Once the car was loaded, they headed out to pick up Kayla. During the ride to the lake, Dad explained the basics of fly fishing. He told Jeremy and Kayla that the sport can be difficult for beginners. "But just like anything, practice makes perfect," he said. They arrived at the lake and started unpacking the fishing equipment.

5. "Uncle Pete, what are those?" Kayla asked, pointing to a very tall pair of boots.

6. "Those are waders," Dad responded. "They protect your feet and legs from getting wet when you're in the water. Let's all put them on."

7. After they all put on their waders, Jeremy let out a big laugh. "We look so goofy in these things!" he said.

8. Dad then prepared three fishing rods for Jeremy, Kayla, and himself. He told them to watch what he was doing so they would learn. A few minutes later, they headed toward the lake. Dad told Jeremy and Kayla to be careful not to fall when entering the lake. They stepped into the water and before they knew it, the water was up to their knees.

9. "Okay guys, watch this," Dad said and cast his line into the water. The line made a perfect loop in the air and landed in the water. Dad then helped Jeremy and Kayla with their casts. It took several attempts for both of them, but eventually they were able to cast their lines into the water, too.

(continued)

(continued)

10. A little while later, Jeremy felt a tug on his line and there was a big splash in the water. "Dad, I think I got one!" Jeremy exclaimed. Dad quickly handed his fishing rod to Kayla so he could help Jeremy. The fishing line was being pulled in all directions, but with Dad's help, Jeremy was able to reel in the fish. Dad reached into the water and gently picked up the fish.

11. "This is a huge trout!" Dad said, handing the fish to Jeremy. Kayla took out a camera and took a picture of Jeremy's big catch.

12. "When I catch my first one, I hope it's as big as yours," Kayla said.

13. Jeremy then released the fish back into the water and smiled. He had found a new hobby that he really liked.

Read and analyze the prompt.

Narrative Prompt

Rewrite the story from Dad's point of view. Be sure to include his thoughts and feelings about the events and other characters. Use details from "Jeremy's Big Catch" in your new story.

COMMON CORE
STATE STANDARD
W.5.3

Read and analyze the model.

Teaching the Kids to Fly-Fish

by Lori Burke

I could not wait until Friday, the day I had planned to teach the kids to fly-fish. After my son Jeremy loaded our fishing gear into the car, we went to pick up my niece, Kayla. The kids were excited. I really wanted them to have a great time and learn to love fly-fishing as much as I do.

As we drove to the river, I explained the basics of fly-fishing to them. I tried to warn them that it can be difficult. I didn't want them to become frustrated.

After we put on our waders, Jeremy laughed. "We look so goofy in these things!" Jeremy said and we all laughed.

I prepared their rods. I was worried that one of the kids would fall when walking into the river. "Watch where you're walking," I warned them. "You can easily trip and fall." They didn't, thank goodness.

Once in the water, I taught them how to cast their lines. They did well! They were off to a great start.

Then Jeremy felt a tug on his line. His eyes were as wide as golf balls. I helped him reel in the fish. It was a huge trout. Kayla took a picture of Jeremy and his fish. "When I catch my first one, I hope it's as big as yours," she said.

I think they both had a great day. I know I did.

✔ Writing Checklist: Narrative

❏ The writer established a setting or situation for her narrative.

❏ The writer introduced a narrator and/or characters.

❏ The writer organized her narrative into a sequence of unfolding events.

❏ The writer used dialogue and description to develop events and show how characters respond to them.

❏ The writer used transitional words to show the sequence of events.

❏ The writer used concrete words and phrases and sensory details to describe events.

❏ The writer wrote a conclusion to the events in her narrative.

❏ The writer reviewed her writing for good grammar.

❏ The writer reviewed her writing for capitalization, punctuation, and spelling.

COMMON CORE
STATE STANDARD
W.5.3

Writing a Narrative

Mini-Lesson 6: **Writing to Multiple Texts**

> **COMMON CORE STATE STANDARD W.5.3**
>
> **Write narratives to develop real or imagined experiences or events using effective technique, descriptive details, and clear event sequences.**
>
> a. Orient the reader by establishing a situation and introducing a narrator and/or characters; organize an event sequence that unfolds naturally.
>
> b. Use narrative techniques, such as dialogue, description, and pacing, to develop experiences and events or show the responses of characters to situations.
>
> c. Use a variety of transitional words, phrases, and clauses to manage the sequence of events.
>
> d. Use concrete words and phrases and sensory details to convey experiences and events precisely.
>
> e. Provide a conclusion that follows from the narrated experiences or events.

Explain to students that they will often encounter writing prompts that instruct them to respond directly to more than one passage. For example, they might have to read two fictional passages by the same author or two informational passages about the same topic. Then take the following steps to guide students through the process of writing a narrative piece in response to multiple texts.

Read the passages. Distribute pages 42–45 to students. Depending on students' needs, you may wish to read the passages aloud, have students read them with a partner, or have them read the passages independently.

Read and analyze the prompt. Read the prompt at the bottom of page 45 with students. Model how to analyze the prompt. Ask questions such as the following:

- *What form of writing does the prompt ask for?* (narrative)

- *How can you tell?* (The prompt asks me to write a sequel to "Paddling to Paradise" in which the narrator of the story meets the speaker of the poem, and they discuss their experiences at the river.)

- What is the purpose(s) of the assignment? (to write a narrative using dialogue)

- What information do I need to complete the task? (I need to use evidence from the story "Paddling to Paradise" and from the poem "Room for Thought.")

Plan the writing. Draw the following graphic organizer on the board. You may also wish to distribute the matching graphic organizer located on page 125. Use the following think-alouds to model how to complete the graphic organizer. Ask for student input as you fill in the chart on the board.

- *The prompt asks me to imagine that the narrator of the story and the speaker of the poem have visited the same river and have seen the same eagles.*

- *The prompt also asks me to write a sequel to "Paddling to Paradise" in which they meet and discuss their experiences. I need to give them names and include dialogue in my story.*

- *I will list the details in the chart below.*

- *To finish my writing, I need a concluding statement or paragraph.*

Main Idea:
The narrator of the story (Tyler) meets the speaker of the poem (Kelly) and they discuss the eagles and their experiences.
Details:
1. They can't believe that they saw eagles. Tyler says he saw one dive near the surface of the water. Kelly says she heard a cry and then saw several of them flying overhead. 2. They talk about how much they both like the river. 3. They say good-bye and hope to see each other there again.

Read and analyze the model. Distribute the student writing model and checklist on pages 46–47 to students. Read it aloud. Discuss with students whether or not the writer was successful at accomplishing this task. Ask them to complete the checklist as you discuss the narrative piece.

COMMON CORE
STATE STANDARD

W.5.3

Read the passages.

Paddling to Paradise

1. One day last summer, my cousin Jesse invited me to go with him on a canoe ride on the river. I didn't want to go because I was sure it would be boring. I didn't want to just sit in a boat all day doing nothing. I wanted to play with my friends. But Jesse is in college, and I don't see him that often. I didn't want to hurt his feelings, so I decided to go.

2. Mom drove me to a boat launch near the bridge at Clarkstown. Jesse was waiting for us when we pulled in. Mom had brought everything she thought I might need, including lunch, a hat, a jacket, and sunscreen.

3. We hauled it all from the car down to the canoe. Jesse put it all into plastic boxes, so it wouldn't get wet. Then he asked me to put on a life jacket.

4. Mom kissed me good-bye and told us to be careful and not to take any chances. We promised to be good. I got into the canoe, and Jesse pushed it out into the river. He jumped in when the water was about knee-deep. He picked up a paddle, and we started off.

5. It was really quiet on the river. We traveled only a short distance when Jesse told me to grab the other paddle, which was on the floor behind me. He showed me how to hold it and push it through the water.

6. It wasn't hard to do since we were moving with the current of the river. After a while, I got into a rhythm and we worked well together.

7. "Look!" Jesse said, pointing at the shore, where three deer were drinking. One was a buck with huge antlers. I wished I had my camera with me.

8. Then, farther down the river, we saw a black bear lumbering over some rocks. He grabbed a fish right out of the water and took off into the woods. It happened so fast that I didn't even have time to be scared.

(continued)

(continued)

9.   Later, we were floating along with the current, and I saw something move above me. A huge bird was flying high in the sky. Suddenly it dove down to the surface of the water. It was a bald eagle! It didn't get a fish, so it flew back up to its perch on an evergreen tree. I couldn't believe that I had actually seen an eagle.

10.   When we reached our meeting place with Mom, Jesse steered us to the shore. Mom looked happy to see us safely back on land, but I wished we could have stayed on the river longer. Jesse promised to take me again the next time he came home.

(continue to next passage)

COMMON CORE
STATE STANDARD
W.5.3

(continued)

Room for Thought

1. I was looking for some open ground
2. to think about my cares.
3. A lot had happened yesterday;
4. it didn't seem quite fair.

5. I walked beyond the city
6. to a woodland wide with space,
7. where I chanced upon a river,
8. and it seemed a peaceful place.

9. I walked along the water's edge
10. and heard a single cry.
11. And looking up, I saw the wings
12. of eagles spread on high.

(continued)

COMMON CORE
STATE STANDARD
W.5.3

(continued)

13. Their beauty and their majesty
14. soon caused my thoughts to lift.
15. As if my hurt had flown away
16. I watched them soar and drift.

17. I walked along the eastern shore
18. And looked into the sun
19. Another day was passing
20. And the healing had begun.

Read and analyze the prompt.

Narrative Prompt

Imagine that the narrative of the story and the speaker of the poem have visited the same river and have seen the same eagles. Write a sequel to the story "Paddling to Paradise" in which they meet and discuss their experiences. Give them names and include dialogue. Base their discussion on the details in the story "Paddling to Paradise" and the poem "Room for Thought."

COMMON CORE
STATE STANDARD

W.5.3

Read and analyze the model.

A New Friend

by Danny Harrison

Before I got into the car with Mom, I saw a girl who looked about my age walking toward us. "Did you see those eagles?" she asked me.

"I saw one. It dove down to the water from an evergreen tree to try to get a fish. It was the most beautiful thing I have ever seen," I explained.

"I heard something—a cry coming from the sky while I was walking. I looked up and saw three of them flying overhead. They were huge! They were just drifting in the air. It was incredible to see them. I'm Kelly," she said and extended her hand.

I shook her hand. "I'm Tyler," I said. I explained that I had never been on the river in a canoe before but that I truly enjoyed it. I told Kelly about the deer I saw and the black bear catching a fish. She told me that she often walks by the river and that she lives nearby.

"I live in that gray house right there," she said and pointed. "I like to walk by the river because it's so calm and peaceful. I can think clearly here."

(continued)

Common Core Writing to Texts Grade 5 • ©2014 Newmark Learning, LLC

(continued)

"Maybe I'll see you again. My cousin Jesse promised to take me on another canoe ride the next time he's in from college."

"You bet," she said. "Feel free to stop by my house. Maybe we can go for a walk together," she said. I told her that I would definitely stop by.

✔ Writing Checklist: Narrative

The writer established a setting or situation for his narrative.

- ❏ The writer introduced a narrator and/or characters.
- ❏ The writer organized his narrative into a sequence of unfolding events.
- ❏ The writer used dialogue and description to develop events and show how characters respond to them.
- ❏ The writer used transitional words to show his sequence of events.
- ❏ The writer used concrete words and phrases and sensory details to describe events.
- ❏ The writer wrote a conclusion to the events in his narrative.
- ❏ The writer reviewed his writing for good grammar.
- ❏ The writer reviewed his writing for capitalization, punctuation, and spelling.

Practice Texts with Prompts

How to Use Practice Texts with Prompts

This section of Writing to Texts provides opportunities for students to practice writing frequently in a wide range of genres and provides authentic practice for standardized writing assessments. Each practice lesson contains a passage or pair of passages followed by three prompts.

Before beginning, assign students one of the prompts, or ask them each to choose one. Explain to students that they are to plan and write an essay about the passage or passages according to the instructions in the chosen prompt. They should write on a separate piece of paper, or in a writing journal designated for writing practice.

There are various ways to use the practice section. You may wish to have students complete the writing tasks at independent workstations, as homework assignments, or as test practice in a timed environment.

If you choose to use these as practice for standardized tests, assign one prompt and give students 60 minutes to execute the task. In using these as test practice, tell students that they should think of their writing as a draft, and tell them they will not have additional time to revise their work.

You may also choose to have students respond to the prompts orally to strengthen academic oral language skills.

Graphic organizers for each type of writing are included on pages 120–125. You may choose to distribute them to help students plan and organize. On pages 126–127, reproducible Student Writing Checklists are provided. Distribute them to students to serve as checklists as they write, or as self-assessment guides.

Conducting Research

The Common Core State Standards require that students are provided opportunities to learn research techniques and to apply these skills in their preparation of projects. The passages in this section can make for research project starters. After students respond to an informational prompt, ask them to conduct further research on information from the practice text in order to build their knowledge.

Explain to students that researchers take good notes, connect new knowledge to what is already known, organize information into sensible layouts for a report, cite their sources, and use their own words to convey the information.

Tell students to gather information from print and digital sources. Have them take brief notes on sources and sort their facts, details, and evidence into categories. They may choose an appropriate organizer from pages 120–125.

Practice Texts with Prompts Table of Contents

COMMON CORE
STATE STANDARDS

W.5.1–
W.5.10

Name_____ Date_____

Read the passage below.

Advantage on the Field

1. Kim joined the back row of ten-year-old girls and followed the assistant coach's lead, gently stretching and jogging in place to warm up. Twenty-four girls her age were trying out for the soccer team, and they all seemed eager to begin.

2. Kim had prepared for tryouts all summer and decided that her chances were good. She had jogged with her mother to build endurance and practiced goal kicks with her father, so she was confident that she had an advantage.

3. Though Kim didn't think she had much athletic ability, she enjoyed playing soccer with her older brothers. When she learned about the soccer league tryouts, Kim decided to challenge herself and attempt to make a team.

4. Kim hoped she could demonstrate the skills she'd learned from playing soccer with her brothers. Coach Walsh was in charge of the tryouts. She took notes as the girls ran passing drills. A few girls soon seemed exhausted by the effort of the brisk exercises, and Kim congratulated herself on not tiring.

5. The coaches were deep in conversation when the young athletes took a brief rest. Kim drank water and wiped sweat from her face, concentrating on her family in the stands. Afterward, the coaches divided the girls into two teams for a scrimmage, or practice game. Kim slipped on a red shirt. She nimbly passed the ball to one of her teammates and the reds quickly scored.

6. As the minutes passed, Kim applied pressure to the opposing team to gain possession of the ball. She became concerned because she had no opportunities to take the ball to the net. Kim kept passing to her teammates, but felt she wasn't achieving her goal of showing the coaches her valuable skills.

(continued)

Name_____ Date_____

COMMON CORE
STATE STANDARDS
W.5.1–
W.5.10

(continued)

7.   Coach Walsh halted the scrimmage by blowing her whistle. "Please take a seat on the front row of the stands," said her assistant. "Coach Walsh will have the results in a few minutes."

8.   Kim decided that her tryout had been a disaster. She perched glumly on the bench, ready to bolt to hide her disappointment at not being chosen.

9.   Kim was astounded when Coach Walsh called her name. The coach thanked the girls who were not chosen and then distributed practice schedules to the team.

10.   Coach Walsh noticed that Kim hesitated before taking her schedule. "Change your mind?" the coach asked, smiling.

11.   "I didn't think I'd made it," Kim said, perplexed by the development. "I didn't even score."

12.   Coach Walsh nodded. "That's true, but I'm looking for players who cooperate," she explained. "Independence is valuable, but on the soccer field, I need excellent team players like you."

13.   Kim smiled at the compliment. "Thanks, Coach Walsh," she said, eager now to celebrate her success with her parents and brothers. "See you at practice!"

COMMON CORE
STATE STANDARDS
W.5.1–
W.5.10

Name_____ Date_____

Opinion/Argument Prompt

Do you think it's more important to score or to cooperate when you're a member of a team? Why? Support your opinion with details from the text and your own ideas.

Informative/Explanatory Prompt

Kim thinks her tryout was a disaster. Was it a disaster? Why or why not? Use specific details from the text to summarize Kim's performance at tryouts.

Narrative Prompt

Imagine that you were one of the girls who did not make the team. Write a story about tryouts and Kim's performance from this girl's point of view.

Name_____ Date_____

COMMON CORE
STATE STANDARDS
W.5.1–
W.5.10

Read the passage below.

Pandora's Box

1.   Long before man was created, Earth was ruled by a group of gods and a race of giants. One of the giants, named Prometheus, created man and made him smarter and more skilled than any animal. Zeus, the king of the gods, did not like man and did not want him to be better than the animals.

2.   One day, Prometheus stole fire from the home of the gods and gave it to man. Zeus was furious. He did not want man to have fire, and he was angry that Prometheus dared to steal from the gods. He decided he would soon get back at Prometheus by punishing man.

3.   Zeus asked one of his fellow gods to create a female human. She was made out of clay and given different qualities by each of the gods. They gave her beauty, grace, and talent. They also gave her curiosity. When she was finished, she was given the name Pandora and became the first woman on Earth and wife of Prometheus's brother, Epimetheus.

4.   Zeus also sent Pandora to Earth with a special gift. He gave her and Epimetheus a heavy golden box with a big lock on it. He told them that they were never to open the box for any reason and gave Pandora's husband the key for safekeeping.

5.   Because the gods had given her curiosity, Pandora really wanted to know what was inside the box. She studied it every day and imagined what wonders it held. She begged Epimetheus to open it, but he refused to disobey Zeus.

6.   One day, while Epimetheus was sleeping, Pandora decided that she could no longer control her curiosity. She just had to know what was in the box! She quietly took the key from her husband's room and snuck off to where the box was kept.

(continued)

Name_____ Date_____

(continued)

7. When she unlocked and opened the box, Pandora did not receive the surprise she expected. As she lifted the lid, many evil beings flew out. Anger, hate, jealousy, and disease, which were never before part of life on Earth, entered the world for the first time.

8. Pandora felt terrible. She knew that because of her the world was now full of evil and hardship. Her actions made life all but unbearable for humans everywhere. She was ashamed and saddened.

9. Suddenly, Pandora felt a warmth that eased her pain and made her feel better about herself. She peered into the box again and saw that there was one more thing just beginning to float out. It was hope. Pandora was overjoyed. Though the world was filled with many bad things, it also had hope.

Name_____ Date_____

COMMON CORE
STATE STANDARDS
W.5.1–
W.5.10

Opinion/Argument Prompt

Do you think Zeus's method of punishing Prometheus was fair? Support your opinion with details from the text.

Informative/Explanatory Prompt

What can you tell about Prometheus from the story? Use details from the text to support your explanation.

Narrative Prompt

Rewrite the story from Pandora's point of view. Tell how she feels about the locked box and how she feels when things come out of the box.

COMMON CORE
STATE STANDARDS
W.5.1–
W.5.10

Name_____ Date_____

Read the passage below.

The Sword in the Stone

1.   Many, many years ago in the kingdom of Britain lived a wizard named Merlin. Upon the death of the king, Merlin took a sword and thrust it into a large stone that lay in a clearing of the forest. He then declared that whoever could remove it would be the next king. Many knights tried their hand at removing it, but none succeeded. The sword remained where it was put, and there was no king for the people all the while.

2.   At that time their lived a young boy named Wart who knew nothing of this sword or of Merlin's words. Wart was the son of Sir Ector, one of the great knights of the kingdom. He lived in Sir Ector's castle along with his older brother, Kay.

3.   Though Wart and Kay were good friends, they weren't always able to spend much time together. As Sir Ector's oldest son, Kay was expected to follow in his father's footsteps and train to become a knight himself.

4.   While Kay was training, Wart would wander about exploring the forest. On one such occasion, Wart stayed out wandering longer than usual and traveled so far from the castle that he couldn't find his way home before the sun set and all fell into darkness. He was lost!

5.   As Wart struggled to find his way back to the castle, he suddenly heard a strange voice behind him.

6.   "Hello, young traveler," said the voice. Wart swung around and saw an old man with a long white beard dressed in flowing robes. "I am the wizard Merlin," said the man. "I will help you find your way."

7.   As they walked, Merlin offered to teach Wart the ways of nature and life. Wart agreed and learned a great deal about virtue and leadership from the wizard.

(continued)

Common Core Writing to Texts Grade 5 • ©2014 Newmark Learning, LLC

Name_____ Date_____

(continued)

8.   By the time Wart returned home, Kay had become a knight and Wart was required to be his servant. For his part, Wart still loved his brother and didn't mind being treated like second best. Little did he know that this would soon change.

9.   One day, a great tournament was held to determine, finally, who would be the next king. To Wart's surprise, Merlin was at the tournament, standing in the shadows.

10.   All the knights attended in full armor and competed on horseback against one another. During the tournament, Kay broke his sword and ordered Wart to return home and get another. Wart did as he was instructed, but he couldn't find another sword anywhere.

11.   Wart decided to cut through the forest to get back to the tournament. It was there that he came upon the sword in the stone. He didn't realize that this was a special sword, but he was grateful to find *any* sword at all for Kay. Giving it one firm pull, Wart easily removed the sword from the rock and took it to his brother.

12.   When Kay and the others realized which sword Wart had come back with, they fell to their knees before him. At that moment, Merlin came forward and revealed that Wart had been adopted by Sir Ector and that his real father was the late king. He also announced that Wart's real name was Arthur and that he was now the king of England.

COMMON CORE
STATE STANDARDS

W.5.1–
W.5.10

Name_____ Date_____

Opinion/Argument Prompt

Do you think Kay will be jealous of Wart now that Wart is king? Do you think Kay will obey him? Why or why not? Support your opinion with details and quotations from the text.

Informative/Explanatory Prompt

When Wart meets Merlin, Merlin says "I will help you find your way." What do you think Merlin means by this? Support your explanation with details from the text.

Narrative Prompt

Rewrite the story from Merlin's point of view. Base your story on the details in the text, but include your own ideas as well.

Name_____ Date_____

COMMON CORE
STATE STANDARDS
W.5.1–
W.5.10

Read the passage below.

Helping the Hippos

1. The Kovac family was standing at their upstairs window, looking out over the city of Budapest, Hungary. Their faces were full of worry. It was the winter of 1944, and World War II had been raging for years. Now, both German and Russian armies were fighting for control of Budapest.

2. Eleven-year-old Adela Kovac squinted to see through the swirling snow outside. "Look, Grandpa," she said. "The Germans are on one side of the city and the Russians are on the other."

3. "Only the Danube River is between them, keeping them from fighting," said Grandpa.

4. Adela's little brother Jakob suddenly gasped so hard his favorite straw hat almost fell off. "Think what else is right between them," he said. "The zoo!"

5. The mention of the Budapest Zoo sent the family into a daydream. They remembered happier times, before the war, when they'd gone to the zoo together. Their favorite animals, the hippopotamuses, had enjoyed bathing in the local warm springs and munching on grass. The idea that the zoo might be in danger made the Kovacs feel even more heartsick.

6. "Can we take some food to the hippos?" said Adela.

7. Mother frowned and said, "Sweetheart, we can't do much to help them. With all the trouble in the city, it's hard enough getting food to feed our family."

8. But Grandpa rubbed his bristly chin and said, "Hippopotamuses wouldn't want our food anyway. They eat grass and straw."

(continued)

COMMON CORE
STATE STANDARDS
W.5.1–
W.5.10

Name_____ Date_____

(continued)

9. "The army horses probably ate most of the grass, and the rest is covered in snow," said Jakob sadly. "Where can we find straw?"

10. Even though Adela was upset, she had to laugh. "How about your silly straw hat?" she said.

11. Jakob took off his hat. "I love this hat, but I'd sacrifice it."

12. Grandpa said, "One hat isn't going to do it. Go gather the straw floor mats in the kitchen."

13. Mother added, "You can take my straw slippers as well."

14. Now Adela and Jakob ran through the house, piling every piece of straw they could find into a wheelbarrow. With Grandpa's help, they headed through the streets to the zoo. Some Russian soldiers laughed at the strange sight, but let them pass.

15. Adela and Jakob found the hippos looking hungry. Jakob tossed out his beloved hat and one of the huge animals eagerly chomped on it. Soon, the animals were gathering for a tasty meal.

16. They emptied the wheelbarrow quickly. All the straw in the house had been eaten. The children felt discouraged, but they noticed that the hippos were still gathered. Curious, the children turned around. To their surprise and delight, they saw the pathway filled with neighbors wheeling down their own carts full of straw!

17. Adela and Jakob hugged each other with glee. With all the suffering of the awful war, this was at least a sign that hope was still alive and that a better tomorrow lay ahead.

Name_____ Date_____

COMMON CORE
STATE STANDARDS
W.5.1–
W.5.10

 Opinion/Argument Prompt

The last sentence of the story says, "With all the suffering of the awful war, this was at least a sign that hope was still alive and that a better tomorrow lay ahead." After reading this story, do you agree with this statement? Why or why not? Support your opinion with details from the text and your own ideas.

 Informative/Explanatory Prompt

Why is the Kovac family worried about the hippos? Use details from the text to support your explanation.

 Narrative Prompt

Imagine that you are one of the Russian soldiers who let Grandpa, Adela, and Jakob pass. Write a journal entry that this solder might have recorded after the experience.

COMMON CORE
STATE STANDARDS
W.5.1–
W.5.10

Name_____ Date_____

Read the passage below.

The BFF History Project

1. *Setting: A girl's bedroom with the pillow-covered bed center stage. Many photos and items are tacked onto a bulletin board, and books line a shelf. Rain falls beyond the window.*

2. *(Two eleven-year-old girls enter the room and throw themselves across the bed.)*

3. **Fay:** Well, so much for our big plans for our last weekend together. This rain is supposed to last for days.

4. **Isabel:** I'm not worried. The rain can't cancel our sleepover, and I prepared for this weekend. *(She reaches under the bed and pulls out a box.)*

5. **Fay:** For me? Thank you!

6. **Isabel:** *(laughing)* For both of us! Mom has been helping me print out photos of all the things our families have done together, and your mother gave me a collection of souvenirs recently. *(Isabel opens the box and pours the contents onto the bed.)* I thought we could create a time capsule.

7. **Fay:** *(laughing)* A BFF history project! You're making me do homework! *(She picks up some of the items on the bed.)* Oh, that's a ticket from the school play. Acting was exciting, even though I had to wear a mustache because we didn't have enough boys in the cast.

8. **Isabel:** Your mom saved the mustache. *(sticks mustache onto Fay's face)* Remember this? *(shows photo)* We made friendship bracelets during that camping trip when we were seven. It rained all weekend then, too. I wore my bracelet until it practically dissolved.

9. **Fay:** Every summer since then, we've braided new ones. *(holds out her arm)* We should make some tonight. This one's getting pretty worn.

(continued)

Name_____ Date_____

COMMON CORE
STATE STANDARDS
W.5.1–
W.5.10

(continued)

10. **Isabel:** Mine is, too. *(She rises from the bed, unpins a card from the bulletin board, and sits beside Fay.)* Do you remember this card? You made it for me when I had a cold and missed the first day of kindergarten. Mom thought you drew a turtle! *(both girls laugh)* I could tell it was your cat. You're still better at drawing than I am.

11. **Fay:** *(sitting up)* That was the only first day of school when we weren't together. I won't know anyone in the new neighborhood. School starts in a month, and I'm already nervous. Mom's new job and our new house are so far away.

12. **Isabel:** We'll call each other. You'll start school the day before I will, so you can tell me all about it when you get home. I'll call you after my first day. This history box—our history—isn't over.

13. **Fay:** We'll be back for Thanksgiving dinner with my grandparents. That weekend, our families are seeing a show at the community theater together.

14. **Isabel:** The BFF history project, to be continued!

15. *(As the girls laugh and hug, the curtain falls.)*

COMMON CORE
STATE STANDARDS
W.5.1–
W.5.10

Name_____ Date_____

Opinion/Argument Prompt

Do you think looking at photos of the past and souvenirs is a fun activity to do with a friend on a rainy day? Support your opinion with details from the text and your own ideas.

Informative/Explanatory Prompt

What is Fay's problem, and how does Isabel try to help her solve it? Use details from the text to support your explanation.

Narrative Prompt

Write a story about the BFF history project from Fay's point of view. Use details from the play in your story.

Name_____ Date_____

Read the passage below.

Jacques Cousteau

1.   Jacques-Yves Cousteau dedicated his life to helping people learn about the sea. He was born in a small village in France on June 11, 1910. Cousteau was a sickly child, but his parents insisted that he learn how to swim at a young age. Little did they realize how important this would be to Cousteau—and the world—later in his life!

2.   As he grew up, Cousteau was not a good student. However, he was smart and quite curious about things that interested him. For example, as a teenager, he took apart a movie camera because he wanted to know how it worked.

3.   In 1933, Cousteau was nearly killed in a car accident. To recover from his injuries, he started to swim in the Mediterranean Sea each day. A friend lent him a pair of goggles so he could get a closer look at the sea creatures. Cousteau began to study sea life very closely at this time.

4.   During World War II, Cousteau met an engineer named Emile Gagnan. Emile was also interested in the sea. Because they wanted to study life underwater, Cousteau and Gagnan worked on a system that would allow them to stay under the water for longer times. Their first "aqua-lung" device was a success.

5.   Around this time, Cousteau also helped develop a camera that worked underwater. These two inventions helped Cousteau to film his first two documentaries, or fact-based films, about the sea.

6.   In 1950, Cousteau turned a British sea vessel into a research ship and named it the *Calypso*. Working with the National Geographic Society, Cousteau used the *Calypso* to film several more films about the sea.

(continued)

COMMON CORE
STATE STANDARDS
W.5.1–
W.5.10

Name_____ Date_____

(continued)

7. His television series, *The Undersea World of Jacques Cousteau*, was launched in 1968. This program ran for nine years and helped millions of people learn a great deal about marine life.

8. Through his work, Cousteau began to see how human activity was hurting the oceans. He became an environmental activist, a person who raises awareness about issues that harm the environment.

9. Over the next few decades, Cousteau wrote several books and made many films. He worked hard to get his message about the oceans to as many people as possible. He founded the Cousteau Society in 1973 to raise money and awareness all around the world.

10. In January 1996, the *Calypso* was accidentally destroyed when it was hit by a larger ship. Cousteau began raising funds to build a new ship. Before he could make that happen, he died unexpectedly on June 25, 1997. He was 87 years old. The world was saddened by his death, but grateful for his many contributions to science.

Name_____ Date_____

Opinion/Argument Prompt

What do you think was Jacques Cousteau's greatest achievement? Why? Support your opinion with facts and quotations from the text.

Informative/Explanatory Prompt

In the first paragraph, the author says that Cousteau "dedicated his life to helping people learn about the sea." Use other facts from the text to explain why this is true.

Narrative Prompt

Write a journal entry Cousteau may have recorded after he met Emile Gagnan. Use facts from the passage.

Name_____ Date_____

Read the passage below.

Make a Bouncing Egg

1.   An egg is a very fragile object. If someone drops or even just bumps an uncooked egg, the egg's outer shell can break, and its contents can spill out. Even after an egg has been cooked, it is still quite delicate and has a shell that can be easily cracked. However, there is a way to make an egg that can actually bounce!

2.   To create a bouncing egg, a few items are needed. Gather together these three items: a fresh, raw egg; a bottle of white vinegar; and a clear glass jar. The best type of jar to use is a small jelly jar.

3.   Make sure that the jar has a tight-fitting lid. Also, the egg will need to be boiled, so ask an adult to help with the first part of this experiment.

4.   With an adult supervising the process, boil the egg on the stove in a pot of water. Sometimes people add salt to water when they boil eggs, but that is not necessary for this experiment.

5.   Allow the egg to boil for about ten minutes. Once the egg has finished boiling, turn off the stove and allow the egg to cool off for a few minutes.

6.   Now, take the cool boiled egg and place it inside the glass jar with care. Try not to drop the egg, as that will cause the shell to crack. One way to get the egg into the jar is to put it on a spoon and carefully slide the spoon down the inside of the glass.

(continued)

Name_____ Date_____

COMMON CORE
STATE STANDARDS
W.5.1–
W.5.10

(continued)

7.   Once the egg is resting safely on the bottom of the jar, pour the white vinegar into the jar until the egg is entirely covered in vinegar.

8.   Then, carefully place the lid on the jar and close it very tightly. Put the jar in a safe place and leave it there for one week.

9.   After one week has passed, open the lid and drain the vinegar from the jar. Take the egg out of the jar and rinse it off with some cool tap water. Pat it dry carefully. The egg should feel rubbery, just like a ball. Try dropping it on a flat surface, and watch it bounce!

A Quick Guide to Making a Bouncing Egg

- Boil a raw egg in water and let it cool.
- Place the egg at the bottom of a small glass jar.
- Cover the egg with white vinegar and close the jar with a lid.
- Set the jar aside for one week.
- Drain the vinegar and bounce the egg!

COMMON CORE
STATE STANDARDS

W.5.1–
W.5.10

Name_____ Date_____

 Opinion/Argument Prompt

Do you think the egg would bounce if you put water in the jar instead of white vinegar? Why or why not? State your claim and support your argument with details from the text and your own ideas.

 Informative/Explanatory Prompt

Imagine that you have made a bouncing egg. Explain how this egg is different from a raw egg. Use facts and details from the text to support your explanation.

 Narrative Prompt

Write a story about two characters who try to make a bouncing egg, but it cracks when they bounce it. Have them discuss what they may have done wrong. Give your characters names and include dialogue in the story.

 Common Core Writing to Texts Grade 5 • ©2014 Newmark Learning, LLC

Name_____ Date_____

COMMON CORE
STATE STANDARDS
W.5.1–
W.5.10

Read the passage below.

Festival in the Sky

1.   I've been really excited ever since my mom told my sister Maggie and me that she would take us to the Adirondack Balloon Festival this year. Mom knows how much I enjoy outdoor events, and she was eager to tell us about the amazing collection of hot air balloons we would see on the fairgrounds. She said they would be in all shapes and sizes. We would get to learn how the balloons work and how they are made. We would even get to see a very special event called the Moon Glow!

2.   Although I was delighted about the festival, Maggie wasn't so sure. She had seen a hot air balloon at the zoo one time and was scared by its flames and loud noises. She didn't seem very happy about going to the festival.

3.   Our drive to Glens Falls took us more than three hours from New York City. But the excitement of what was to come made the time fly by. As our car wove in and out on the beautiful mountainside road, I pictured all sorts of beautiful balloons drifting through the air.

4.   Before I knew it, we pulled into a giant open field at Crandall Park. As we walked through the crowd of people to the main entrance, Maggie looked nervous but interested. I was just plain excited.

5.   Once we made our way inside the gates, we had the chance to see the balloons up close. They were scattered all around the enormous field.

(continued)

COMMON CORE
STATE STANDARDS

W.5.1–
W.5.10

Name_____ Date_____

(continued)

6.   Many were decorated with brilliant rainbow patterns. One looked like a giant strawberry! There were unusual shapes like a giant crab, a soaring butterfly—even a floating birthday cake! Maggie especially liked one that was purple and pink with blue and green swirls. Suddenly, she was all smiles!

7.   We got to meet one of the balloon pilots. He let us climb inside the basket and showed us the burner. He explained that when he turned the burner on, flames warmed up the air inside the balloon. This, he said, made the balloon lighter than the air around it and allowed it to rise. He also told us that most balloons fly as high as 2,000 feet and some have traveled nearly 8,000 miles.

8.   We had a blast eating festival food and looking at the different sites. When day turned to night, the Moon Glow began. Everyone watched in awe as the balloons began to glow in the dark.

9.   Slowly, the great balloons inched off the ground and floated up through the air. Soon the whole sky was filled with giant balls of light. I enjoyed every minute of it—and glancing over, I saw that Maggie did, too.

Common Core Writing to Texts Grade 5 • ©2014 Newmark Learning, LLC

Name_____ Date_____

COMMON CORE
STATE STANDARDS
W.5.1–
W.5.10

Opinion/Argument Prompt

Do you think a balloon festival is a good place to go on a school field trip? Why or why not? Support your opinion with facts and quotations from the text.

Informative/Explanatory Prompt

Explain the importance of a burner in making a hot air balloon fly. Use facts and quotations from the text to support your explanation.

Narrative Prompt

Rewrite the text as a story from Maggie's point of view. Have her describe how and why her feelings about having to attend the balloon festival change.

COMMON CORE
STATE STANDARDS
**W.5.1–
W.5.10**

Name_____ Date_____

Read the passage below.

The Maasai People of Africa

1.   In the modern era, many tribal peoples struggle to preserve their traditional way of life. These people find it difficult to uphold ancient customs when the world around them is changing. Some tribes are more successful than others.

2.   The Maasai of Africa is one such tribe. The Maasai have successfully preserved their ancient traditions for hundreds of years, despite the many modern developments surrounding them.

3.   The Maasai live on the borders of Kenya and Tanzania in southeastern Africa. They are a nomadic tribe, so they move from place to place as they follow cattle. Cattle are an essential part of Maasai life. The Maasai use cattle for food, milk, shelter, and clothing. They also sell cattle so that they can buy food and medicine.

4.   The Maasai measure wealth in cattle. A Maasai family is considered poor if it owns fewer than 50 cattle and rich if it owns more than 1,000 cattle. Some families give their cattle names and can even identify individual animals by their voices.

5.   The Maasai maintain a traditional appearance. They favor the color red because they believe it stands for power. They use red clay to dye their hair, beards, and clothing. Men grow their hair long and color it red. Women and children, however, shave their heads. Both men and women pierce their ears and wear large hoop earrings and other beaded jewelry.

(continued)

Name_____ Date_____

COMMON CORE
STATE STANDARDS
**W.5.1–
W.5.10**

(continued)

6. Because the Maasai are always on the move, their villages are built as temporary settlements. Maasai women build the homes in each village. Homes are made of sticks and grass and held together with mud and cow dung.

7. Women also add a wall of tree branches around the settlement. This wall encloses the cattle and keeps them safe from predators.

8. As Africa continues to modernize, the governments of Kenya and Tanzania have established programs to encourage the Maasai to abandon their nomadic lifestyle. Some Maasai have followed these programs and found new ways to live and support themselves.

9. Many Maasai, however, prefer the traditional path. As a result, the governments have also introduced new programs to preserve Maasai traditions while educating the people about the modern world.

COMMON CORE
STATE STANDARDS
W.5.1–
W.5.10

Name_____ Date_____

Opinion/Argument Prompt

Do you think the Maasai should abandon their traditional ways in favor of a more modern lifestyle? Why or why not? Support your opinion with facts from the text.

Informative/Explanatory Prompt

How are cattle important to the Maasai? Use facts and quotations from the text to support your explanation.

Narrative Prompt

Write a story about a Maasai boy or girl who is about your age. Tell what this character does during the course of a day. Use details from the text and your own ideas.

Name_____ Date_____

Read the passage below.

Natural Mimics

1. Animal and plant species evolve in different ways to survive in nature. When animals and plants evolve, they change over time. One of the most fascinating ways a species can evolve is by becoming a mimic.

2. A mimic is a plant or an animal that takes on the appearance of another plant or animal. The model, or the species that is being copied, is usually poisonous.

3. Scientists believe that mimics develop the features of another species to become less interesting to predators. (In other words, the mimic is trying to avoid getting eaten!) Predators stay away from the mimic because they think the mimic is poisonous. As a result, the mimic population is better able to survive in the wild.

4. A good example of this can be found among snakes. The Arizona coral snake is a highly poisonous species. This snake lives in different parts of Arizona and New Mexico. The Arizona coral snake has a black head and distinctive body markings. Its body has large rings of red and black mixed with smaller rings of white and yellow.

5. The Arizona coral snake is not a large snake. An adult is only about 21 inches long. But don't be fooled by its small size! Even large predators have learned to avoid this snake because its venom is very strong. In fact, the Arizona coral snake's venom is as powerful as a cobra's!

(continued)

COMMON CORE
STATE STANDARDS
**W.5.1–
W.5.10**

Name_____ Date_____

(continued)

6.   Another snake species looks quite similar to the Arizona coral snake. That's the coral king snake. This nonpoisonous snake has a black head like the Arizona coral snake and has similar rings of black, white, and red on its body. However, it is larger than the Arizona coral snake, growing to 44 inches in length.

7.   The coral king snake lives throughout the Southwest, but it lives in many of the same places as the Arizona coral snake. Because the coral king snake is not poisonous, it is mostly harmless to predators.

8.   Scientists think that the coral king snake changed over time to look like the Arizona coral snake. Taking on the color of the Arizona coral snake helps keep the coral king snake from being eaten by predators. Coral king snakes are more likely to thrive in the wild because predators pass them by.

Name_____ Date_____

COMMON CORE
STATE STANDARDS
**W.5.1–
W.5.10**

Opinion/Argument Prompt

In the first paragraph, the author says that "one of the most fascinating ways a species can evolve is by becoming a mimic." Do you agree with this statement? Why or why not? Support your opinion with facts and quotations from the text.

Informative/Explanatory Prompt

Compare and contrast the Arizona coral snake and the coral king snake. Use facts from the text to support your explanation.

Narrative Prompt

Based on the information in "Natural Mimics," write a story in which a character sees a coral king snake and thinks it's an Arizona coral snake. Have another character explain that the coral king snake is a mimic.

COMMON CORE
STATE STANDARDS
W.5.1–
W.5.10

Name_____ Date_____

Read the passages.

Double the Fun

1. "Guess what?" Alexa exclaimed. "I'm getting my own puppy!"

2. "That's fabulous! When?" asked her best friend, Mia. Mia adored dogs, and her family had two: Linus and Charlie. They were big, gentle dogs that were nearly always well behaved.

3. "Next week, for my birthday," said Alexa. "We're having a family meeting tonight to decide on a breed because puppies can be really expensive, and we have to be practical about choosing one."

4. "Linus and Charlie weren't expensive," said Mia. "We adopted them from an animal shelter. They belonged to an old man who couldn't walk them anymore, so he had to give them up. We were really glad we found them because they're super pets."

5. "Wow, that's a good idea," said Alexa. "I'll bring that up at our family meeting."

6. After dinner, Alexa, her parents, and her brother, Andrew, gathered in the living room.

7. "Well, I don't want a dog," said Andrew, "I want a cat. They're more peaceful and quiet, and they sit on your lap."

8. "I appreciate that," said Dad, "but we'll discuss cats when it's *your* birthday. Alexa is eleven years old now and has consented to take full responsibility for the puppy."

9. "Don't forget," Mom continued, looking at Alexa, "puppies need a lot of attention and care. They have to be fed and exercised often, and they need their messes cleaned up. You have considered that, right Alexa?"

10. "Of course," said Alexa, "But I've been thinking that maybe we shouldn't get a tiny puppy. Mia said they adopted their dogs from an animal shelter and they were already grown and trained—and they weren't expensive. The man who surrendered them even gave the shelter their vet records. I think we should look at the dogs at the shelter first."

(continued)

COMMON CORE
STATE STANDARDS
W.5.1–
W.5.10

Name_____ Date_____

(continued)

11.   Everyone, except Andrew, agreed that it was a good idea. The next Saturday, they went to the local animal shelter, where there were dogs of every size, shape, and color. It was hard to imagine choosing from so many, until a shelter volunteer asked if she could help them. "I'm Cindy," she said. "What kind of dog are you looking for?"

12.   "An obedient dog that's not too large," said Mom.

13.   "I would much rather a cat," said Andrew.

14.   "A beautiful, friendly dog that will play with my friends and me," explained Alexa.

15.   "I think we should get a cat," said Andrew.

16.   Cindy smiled. "It just so happens that last week a family that was moving had to leave behind their dog and cat. They're both very sweet, and we'd love for them to remain together. Would you like to meet them?"

17.   Two hours later, the two new family members were settling into their home. Andrew hugged his yellow cat, Molly, while Alexa took Roscoe, a border collie, out to play in the backyard. Mom sighed. "We didn't plan on two animals," she said, "but it looks like everyone is happy."

(continue to next passage)

COMMON CORE
STATE STANDARDS

W.5.1–
W.5.10

Name_____ Date_____

(continued)

Out to Play

1. "I can't believe my mom is letting me go to the play with you," exclaimed Mia, "and that we get to stay overnight at your cousin Hayley's house!"

2. "It's only a high school play," Alexa reminded her excited friend, "and Hayley won't be home most of the time because she's the star. She has to be at the school to rehearse, and she has plans with her friends after the play." Alexa had been going to Hayley's plays all her life, it seemed, so she wasn't as excited about seeing the play as Mia was. For her, the best part was staying out late and getting to sleep in her cousin Hayley's bunk beds with Mia.

3. After breakfast on Saturday morning, Alexa and her mother picked up Mia and headed for the interstate highway. Alexa's father and brother didn't go because Andrew had choir practice and someone had to take care of their pets, Molly and Roscoe. Alexa and Mia chatted excitedly for the first hour and then settled down to listen to music.

4. Every once in a while, Mia would suddenly sit up and ask a question. "What's the name of the play again?" she asked for the third time. "*Thoroughly Modern Millie*," Alexa repeated patiently. "It's about a girl back in the 1920s who wants to marry her boss. And it's a musical. Hayley plays Millie, of course—she always gets the female lead. She wants to go to acting school after she graduates."

5. Finally, they arrived at Aunt Joanne's house and hauled in their overnight bags. They introduced Mia to Aunt Joanne. Mom and Aunt Joanne gave the girls a snack and began to prepare an early dinner so they wouldn't be late for the play.

6. At 6:30, they piled into Aunt Joanne's minivan and drove to the high school. Alexa admired Hayley and hoped to one day have the courage to try out for a play at her own school. *How does she remember all those lines and songs, especially in front of an audience?*, Alexa wondered.

7. They all thought the play was excellent and that Hayley did a marvelous job as Millie. Alexa introduced Mia to Hayley after the play, and Mia complimented Hayley on her acting skills. Then Hayley left to go out with her friends for a celebration.

8. It was late when they returned to Aunt Joanne's house—so late, in fact, that Alexa and Mia fell asleep as soon as they crawled into the bunk beds, despite their plans to stay up all night talking. But they did talk all the way home—about the play, their school, and their plans for the future.

Name_____ Date_____

COMMON CORE
STATE STANDARDS
W.5.1–
W.5.10

Opinion/Argument Prompt

Would you rather visit an animal shelter or watch a high school play? Support your opinion with details from both "Double the Fun" and "Out to Play."

Informative/Explanatory Prompt

What character traits describe Alexa? Use information from both stories.

Narrative Prompt

Write a story in which Hayley visits Alexa's house and Alexa and Mia introduce her to Roscoe and Molly.

COMMON CORE
STATE STANDARDS

W.5.1–
W.5.10

Name_____ Date_____

Read the passages.

The History Project

1.   Seth sighed as his mother pulled her car into Donald Matthews's driveway on Saturday afternoon. Seth still couldn't believe that Mr. Norton, his teacher, had paired him with Donald Matthews for the "History Day" project. Donald was loud and sometimes rowdy during class. Seth had a feeling that Donald wouldn't take the history project seriously at all.

2.   Seth gathered his backpack from the backseat and walked to the front porch. He rang the doorbell, and a minute later a woman opened the door. Two identical little girls, no more than two years old, clung to her legs.

3.   "You must be Seth. I'm Mrs. Matthews," she said. "Welcome to our home." She waved to Seth's mom as Seth stepped inside the house.

4.   Just then, three boys carrying buckets of water balloons stampeded past Seth. Two barking dogs followed quickly behind them. The barking continued outside and soon blended with shrieks of laughter as the boys launched water balloons at one another. Meanwhile, loud music blasted from a room on the second floor. In the living room, an older boy watched television with the volume blaring. The two little girls attached to Mrs. Matthews's legs began to whimper. Seth stood in stunned silence for a minute.

5.   Mrs. Matthews laughed. "Not used to all this chaos, are you?" she asked. "Mr. Matthews and I have eight children and two dogs, so there's never a dull moment around here."

6.   "Wow," breathed Seth. "At my house, it's just my parents and me."

7.   A typical Saturday at Seth's house was nearly silent. His parents occasionally murmured to each other about stories in the newspaper during breakfast.

(continued)

Name_____ Date_____

COMMON CORE
STATE STANDARDS
W.5.1–
W.5.10

(continued)

8.   Often Dad left to run errands while Mom worked in the garden. Seth usually read books in the den or on the porch swing. The only sounds around him were the ticking of a clock and the occasional purring of his cat.

9.   As Seth walked through Donald's house, he began to understand why Donald was so loud during class. Crying toddlers, laughing little boys, barking dogs, loud music—the noise in his house was constant. How else would Donald's voice ever be heard if he wasn't loud? And his clowning around in the classroom? That was nothing compared with the constant racket in his house.

10.   That afternoon, as Seth left Donald's house, he smiled. He and Donald had worked well together and had nearly finished their project. Seth also had developed a new respect for Donald. He could not imagine trying to study and do homework amid the noise and chaos at Donald's house. All the distractions had made it difficult for Seth to concentrate all afternoon.

11.   As Seth stepped into his house, he heard the familiar tick of the clock and nothing else. *Maybe next time, I'll invite Donald here*, he thought.

(continue to next passage)

COMMON CORE ·
STATE STANDARDS

W.5.1–
W.5.10

Name_____ Date_____

(continued)

Someone Else's Shoes

1. My mother's bedroom closet
2. Is filled with pairs of shoes,
3. Sandals, pumps, and loafers—
4. How does she ever choose?

5. I slip my feet into some pumps
6. And take a clumsy stroll,
7. Imagining what life is like
8. In my mother's role.

9. She certainly is busy,
10. Like a bee inside a hive,
11. Taking care of children
12. While working nine to five.

13. I trade the pumps for flip-flops,
14. Which line the closet floor.
15. And ask myself these questions,
16. "Why not just one pair? Why more?"

17. Does she dream of sun and waves
18. And lounging on the shore?
19. Or are they just more comfortable
20. When her feet are really sore?

21. As I dig a little deeper,
22. I reveal a hidden truth
23. My mom was much like me
24. In the days of her youth.

25. For hidden in the corner,
26. Are some well-worn cowboy boots
27. That my mother must have traded in
28. For shiny shoes and suits.

29. It's hard for me to picture her
30. In boots and worn-out jeans.
31. I'll have to ask her questions
32. To find out what this means.

33. But one thing I have learned is
34. You can really change your views
35. By trying to walk a mile
36. In someone else's shoes.

Name_____ Date_____

COMMON CORE
STATE STANDARDS
W.5.1–
W.5.10

 Opinion/Argument Prompt

Do you think the story or the poem better illustrates the theme that you can change your views about a person by learning about his or her life? Support your opinion with reasons from both "The History Project" and "Someone Else's Shoes."

 Informative/Explanatory Prompt

At the end of "Someone Else's Shoes," the author says, "You can really change your views/By trying to walk a mile/In someone else's shoes." Explain what these lines of the poem mean using details from both the poem and the story "The History Project."

 Narrative Prompt

Write a story in which Seth meets the speaker of the poem "Someone Else's Shoes." Give the speaker of the poem a name. Have Seth and the speaker discuss Donald and the speaker's mother. Include dialogue in your story.

COMMON CORE
STATE STANDARDS
W.5.1–
W.5.10

Name_____ Date_____

Read the passages.

How Butterflies Came to Be
(Native American myth)

1.   It was a sunny summer day, and the Creator was watching the children of the village as they played. They ran and laughed and sang.

2.   Yet the Creator's heart was heavy, thinking of the children getting older as the seasons passed. They would forget their games and grow serious with responsibility just as the trees and flowers fade in the winter cold.

3.   The Creator was distracted by the sunlight and shadows dancing on the ground and by a yellow leaf lifted by the wind. The sky was bright blue and the cornmeal the women were grinding was pure white.

4.   He felt better. *I'll make something with these colors*, he thought. *It will lift my heart and make the children smile.*

5.   The Creator had a special bag for gathering such things. He put in blue from the sky, orange from the sun, white from the cornmeal, and black from the shadows. He added green from the pine needles and purple and red from the flowers. Then he added the songs of the birds.

6.   "Come here, children," he said. "I have something for you. It is a surprise. Open it."

7.   He gave one of the children the bag and waited. The girl opened the bag and out flew hundreds of colorful butterflies, fluttering around the children's heads and tasting the nectar of the flowers.

8.   The children could not stop smiling and laughing. They had never seen anything so beautiful.

(continued)

Common Core Writing to Texts Grade 5 • ©2014 Newmark Learning, LLC

Name_____ Date_____

COMMON CORE
STATE STANDARDS
W.5.1–
W.5.10

(continued)

9.   Then the butterflies began to sing, and the children danced in delight. But soon a songbird flew down and perched on the Creator's shoulder.

10.   "You told us these songs were ours, one for each bird," he scolded. "And now you've given them to these silly butterflies of yours. Isn't it enough that they have all the colors of the rainbow?"

11.   The Creator agreed. "I did make each bird a special song, and the songs belong to you. I'm sorry."

12.   So he took away the songs and the butterflies were silent, as they are to this day. But they are beautiful even so.

(continue to next passage)

Common Core
State Standards
W.5.1–
W.5.10

Name_____ Date_____

(continued)

Why Swans Are White (Norse myth)

1.   A long time ago, the land of Asgard was the home of gods. In this land grew a special tree known as Yggdrasil, the tree of the world. It was the biggest and best of all trees. Its branches extended throughout the world and far into the sky.

2.   Next to the tree was a glorious hall where three goddesses known as the Norns lived. These goddesses were the most powerful beings in the world. It was their job to decide the fate of each of the gods. They did this while sitting in the shade under Yggdrasil.

3.   Beside the tree was the sacred well of Urd, from which the Norns took water to pour on Yggdrasil's branches to keep them healthy. They also coated the tree with sparkling sand from outside the well, making the tree shimmer with beauty.

4.   Later, the gods arrived to sit beside the special tree and hold their court. They ruled the people of Earth. Just as the Norns decided the gods' fate, the gods decided the fate of human beings. As they discussed the fate of each person, the gods drank the water from the well of Urd. This water was the purest ever to exist and was meant only for the goddesses and gods of Asgard.

5.   Then one day, after the Norns had returned to their hall and the gods had gone away, two swans flew by. They dropped down from the sky and landed next to the well of Urd. Thirsty because their journey had been long, the swans drank from the sacred pool.

6.   Immediately, their dark and stained feathers were transformed by the pureness of the water. When they gazed upon each other, they were amazed to see that their feathers were now bright white.

7.   Forever after and still today, all the descendants of the swans have been as white as new snow.

Name_____ Date_____

COMMON CORE
STATE STANDARDS
W.5.1–
W.5.10

Opinion/Argument Prompt

Which myth did you enjoy more? Why? Support your opinion with reasons from "How Butterflies Came to Be" and "Why Swans Are White."

Informative/Explanatory Prompt

Compare and contrast the butterflies in "How Butterflies Came to Be" with the swans in "Why Swans Are White." Explain how they are alike and different using details from both texts.

Narrative Prompt

Write a myth explaining why a rainbow appears after it rains. Include the Creator in "How Butterflies Came to Be" and the goddesses in "Why Swans Are White" in your myth.

Name_____ Date_____

Read the passages.

Geography Bee

1. Ten-year-old Livia gripped her pencil tightly. "Okay," she said. "I'm ready."

2. Her eleven-year-old classmate, Tito, opened his folder. "Which river flows through the Grand Canyon from the Rocky Mountains to the Gulf of California?"

3. Livia's eyes widened. "The Colorado!" she answered.

4. "Correct," said Tito. "This river, which also begins in the Rocky Mountains, is the longest river in the United States."

5. Livia quickly replied, "The Missouri!" Tito quizzed his friend on world geography, putting a line through each answer she got wrong. After several questions about rivers, Tito asked about cities, islands, and large bodies of water.

6. "How did I do?" Livia asked Tito as he finished counting her correct answers.

7. "Out of sixty questions, you answered forty-five correctly," Tito replied. He could see Livia was disappointed.

8. "I have to do much better," Livia said. She wanted to become the fifth-grade geography bee champion, win the school bee, and become the county geography bee champion. Livia stayed after school every Wednesday for a study group and sample quiz. Her quiz scores were gradually improving.

9. Tito studied the quiz questions. "You did very well on most of the questions about the United States," he noted. "Let's concentrate on world geography." Tito offered his friend an atlas. "Study the maps while I find more questions," he suggested.

(continued)

Name_____ Date_____

COMMON CORE
STATE STANDARDS
W.5.1–
W.5.10

(continued)

10. For the next three weeks, Tito helped Livia with sample quizzes every weekend. They both began to notice geographical information everywhere. On a city bus, Livia saw an announcement about a river festival and remembered the major cities along the waterway.

11. Tito read a magazine article and thought about the agriculture of the nation the writer described. Each week, Livia's quiz scores improved.

12. Livia felt nervous as she lined up for the fifth-grade geography bee. She breathed deeply and answered each question carefully. Finally, only Livia and her friend Ruth remained. Livia's next question was about the Hoggar Mountains of Algeria, but she couldn't remember anything about the mountain range and knew her answer was incorrect. Ruth answered the question and Livia congratulated her before taking a seat.

13. "I hope you'll join us for a final study group tomorrow, Livia," said their teacher. "The top two students in each grade compete in the school championship on Friday."

14. Livia was shocked. "I didn't know that!" she exclaimed. "I thought only one winner from each grade could compete." Livia grinned, suddenly excited, and turned to Tito. "Can you find some questions about mountain ranges of Africa?" she asked. "I have two more days to study!"

(continue to next passage)

Common Core
State Standards
W.5.1–
W.5.10

Name_____ Date_____

(continued)

The Crow and the Pitcher
(based on Aesop's fable)

1. One warm day, Raven and Crow flew far and wide in search of water. Though they were close to exhaustion, they pressed on until finally they saw a pitcher on a wall.

2. "I believe we will find refreshment in that pitcher," called Raven to his companion. "I have often seen people pouring water from such vessels." The pair cautiously perched in a nearby tree to be certain there was no danger, then flew to the wall and considered the pitcher.

3. "Yes, I see liquid at the bottom," said Crow, peering down the narrow neck of the pitcher. "We have finally found water!" Crow tried to take a drink, but his beak was too short to reach the liquid and he soon gave up.

4. Seeing the problem, Raven poked his beak into the pitcher. His beak was both too short and too wide to reach the water far below, and he abandoned the attempt.

5. "I am strong enough to push the pitcher over," said Raven. "Then we can drink the water." He leaned against the pitcher until Crow called for him to stop.

6. "If the water spills out, it will seep into the ground and we won't be able to drink it," Crow warned. "We need a plan. If we cooperate, I am confident we will succeed."

7. While Crow concentrated on solving their problem, Raven strutted around the pitcher. He quickly lost patience and decided to abandon the effort.

8. "I am desperate for a drink," Raven declared. "I will look for water on my own. Farewell, chum." He flew away, leaving Crow behind.

9. Crow measured the neck of the vessel with his beak. He flew to the ground, selected a pebble, and returned to the wall, where he dropped the pebble into the pitcher. Crow found another pebble and dropped it in. Again and again, he dropped pebbles into the pitcher, and then checked his progress. Crow determined that the water level had risen and continued his task.

10. Finally, after a great deal of effort, Crow saw that the water was near the top of the pitcher. He poked his beak inside and gratefully took a long drink.

Name_____ Date_____

COMMON CORE
STATE STANDARDS
W.5.1–
W.5.10

Opinion/Argument Prompt

Whom do you admire more, Livia in "The Geography Bee" or Crow in "The Crow and the Pitcher"? Support your opinion with details from both texts.

Informative/Explanatory Prompt

Explain how Livia and Crow are alike. Use details from "The Geography Bee" and "The Crow and the Pitcher" to support your explanation.

Narrative Prompt

Write a story in which Livia meets Raven, who still has not found water to drink. What advice would she give him? Include dialogue in your story.

Common Core
State Standards
W.5.1–
W.5.10

Name_____ Date_____

Read the passages.

Snapshot of the City

Chapter 3

1. It took a while to figure out how to operate Uncle Lou's old camera. For a few hours, Jake turned it in his hands, studying its parts and trying to understand how it worked. It didn't look like the new cameras in the stores. This one even had old film that needed to be developed.

2. In time, though, Jake was able to determine how it worked. He liked the idea of using an old camera. It made him feel important, like the great photographers whose pictures he'd seen at the museum. He thought maybe he would even be like the artists he'd studied in Ms. Honda's art class. Now, all he had to do was take some amazingly great pictures!

3. Jake studied his books about photography and saw some great pictures that captured his imagination. He thought about taking pictures of beautiful sunrises, famous people, and events that would change the world. Maybe, someday, his work would be featured in a book of great camera artists. Now excited and eager to start, Jake grabbed his camera and headed outside.

4. His first few pictures were not great. He admitted to himself that he was just learning to use the camera. He took some pictures of trees and birds in the park that he believed would prove forgettable. Later, he headed downtown, thinking of getting some shots of great buildings. Unfortunately, now that he looked carefully, he noticed that most of the buildings were not remarkable. In fact, most looked pretty similar to one another. Jake took a few pictures anyway, just so he wouldn't feel that he'd wasted the trip.

5. As he walked, Jake thought about some of his favorite pictures, which showed interesting people. He liked pictures in which a person's look and expression gave clues about what he or she may have been thinking or feeling. Maybe Jake could take some good ones now. There were plenty of people roving around the downtown. Jake took some pictures of them. He took snapshots of a man washing store windows, a woman handing out flyers, and a truck driver stopping for lunch on the side of the road.

6. Somehow, none of this seemed remarkable, either. Jake put the camera back into its bag. He headed home feeling rather disappointed.

(continued)

Common Core Writing to Texts Grade 5 • ©2014 Newmark Learning, LLC

Name_____ Date_____

(continued)

Chapter 4

1.　The next day, Jake read about how to develop the pictures he'd taken so he could see how they came out. *Maybe they'll look much better when I actually see them developed*, he said to himself. *Or maybe I'll find that some were much better than I remembered.*

2.　With some help from Uncle Lou, Jake developed the pictures. He set them out on the table before him, his eyes eagerly racing over them.

3.　By the time he'd seen them all, though, his face again carried a look of disappointment. The pictures were just as he'd remembered. They looked plain and simple, just regular glimpses of everyday life.

4.　Jake took the developed photos to show his art teacher, Ms. Honda. When he arrived in the art room, though, Ms. Honda was away at a meeting. Jake waited a few minutes but then had to head to his next class. Feeling upset, he dumped his photographs into the garbage can and headed to math.

5.　After math, Jake saw Ms. Honda looking for him. She explained that she found a pile of interesting pictures in her garbage can and was wondering where they came from. "Are these yours, Jake?"

6.　Blushing, a little embarrassed, Jake nodded.

7.　"Why did you throw them away?" asked Ms. Honda, surprised. "They're quite good. I think you did a good job getting a snapshot of the city the way it really is."

8.　"It's not quite what I was trying to do," said Jake. "They're not fancy like the pictures in museums, or the ones we study in class."

(continued)

Common Core
State Standards
W.5.1–
W.5.10

Name_____ Date_____

(continued)

9.   Ms. Honda smiled. "Not all pictures are the same, Jake, and not all of them become world famous!"

10.   She explained that what he had done was a great start and that he was developing his "eye." Now, every time he took pictures, they would get better. "Even this first batch of pictures is very nice," she added. "It's a good first step."

11.   Ms. Honda pointed out some interesting details in the pictures, such as a light rainbow in the background or a hidden smile on a passerby. "If you hadn't taken these pictures, these little details would be lost forever."

12.   Then Ms. Honda handed Jake a flyer for the Middleton County Fair. She said, "I think you should send some of these to the art show at the fair and see what happens."

13.   Jake smiled and felt his heart beat with excitement. He felt that he'd made a good first step after all, but he had a great deal more to do!

Common Core Writing to Texts Grade 5 • ©2014 Newmark Learning, LLC

Name_____ Date_____

COMMON CORE
STATE STANDARDS
W.5.1–
W.5.10

Opinion/Argument Prompt

Do you think Jake's photographs are valuable? Why or why not? Use details from both chapters of the story to support your opinion.

Informative/Explanatory Prompt

Ms. Honda tells Jake that he is developing his "eye." What does she mean by this? Use details from both chapters of the story to support your explanation.

Narrative Prompt

Write Chapter 5 of the story in which Jake submits his photographs to the art show at the Middleton County Fair. Use details from Chapters 3 and 4 to make a smooth transition into Chapter 5.

COMMON CORE
STATE STANDARDS
W.5.1–
W.5.10

Name_____ Date_____

Read the passages.

Microbes

1. Microbes are tiny organisms. They are microscopic, which means that they are so small they can be seen only with a microscope.

2. The word *microbe* is short for *microorganism*. The prefix *micro-* actually means "small." Bacteria, viruses, fungi, and algae are single-celled microbes.

3. Microbes are the oldest form of life on Earth. They have lived on our planet in some form for billions of years. Microbes are everywhere. They are in just about everything. They can be found in the deepest oceans, the darkest soil, and the highest clouds. They are in the food we eat, the water we drink, and the air we breathe. Microbes can even be found on the inside and outside of all living things—including people!

4. Microbes can be either harmful or helpful to people. For example, strep throat is caused by a bacterial infection. These bacteria—microbes—make people sick. Therefore, we think of those microbes as being harmful.

5. On the other hand, some bacteria have a helping relationship with people. A certain kind of bacteria lives inside the digestive tract of all human beings. These bacteria help the body break down food. Therefore, they are considered helpful.

6. People have learned to take advantage of the properties of microbes. For example, a long time ago, people learned that adding yeast to dough makes it rise. The result is delicious bread. We also learned that adding different bacteria to cow's milk can produce different end products such as cheese and yogurt.

(continued)

Name_____ Date_____

COMMON CORE
STATE STANDARDS
W.5.1–
W.5.10

(continued)

7.   Scientists even grow some microbes intentionally to fight other microbes. For example, fungus is used to make penicillin. The discovery of this critically important medicine was a turning point for humankind. Penicillin's amazing ability to fight bacteria such as those that cause strep throat has helped us overcome serious illnesses and greatly improved the quality of life.

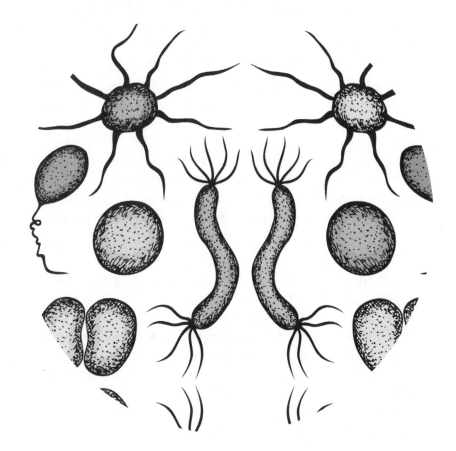

(continue to next passage)

COMMON CORE
STATE STANDARDS
W.5.1–
W.5.10

Name_____ Date_____

(continued)

Microbes: Nature's Waste Cleanup System

1.   Many people believe that microbes are aggressive, deadly creatures that should be destroyed at all costs. And in some cases, they're right. Certain types of microbes can be harmful or deadly to people and the environment.

2.   But don't be so quick to paint all microbes with that "enemy" brush. People and animals can—and do—exist quite peacefully side by side with many different kinds of microbes. Some of these microbes can even be looked on with a friendly eye!

3.   Think for a minute about the amount and type of waste that is generated every day. Consider the amount of waste that leaves one house each week, and then multiply it by the number of houses on a block, in a neighborhood, and in a city. It's a staggering amount of waste. And it doesn't appear that people will reduce the amount of waste they produce anytime soon. This means that we need to do a better job of getting rid of waste. We can't just throw it in a landfill and hope for the best.

4.   What does this have to do with microbes? Well, some microbes can be very deadly—to waste. Scientists have discovered that when they introduce certain type of microbes to problem areas, such as oil spills, the microbes do something amazing. They break down problem compounds such as oil and water and turn them into harmless substances, such as water and carbon dioxide. And, unlike chemical solutions to waste cleanup, the microbes don't produce toxic by-products. That means they aren't harmful to people, animals, or the environment. Microbes are a natural waste recycler that cost little, do the job well, and don't cause more problems than they solve.

Name_____ Date_____

COMMON CORE
STATE STANDARDS
W.5.1–
W.5.10

Opinion/Argument Prompt

The author of "Microbes: Nature's Waste Cleanup System" says that "Many people believe that microbes are aggressive, deadly creatures that should be destroyed at all costs." Why do you think those people feel this way about microbes? Support your opinion with details from both texts and your own ideas.

Informative/Explanatory Prompt

What are some ways that people have used microbes to benefit themselves and the environment? Support your explanation with details from both texts.

Narrative Prompt

Write a story in which a scientist who researches microbes gives a presentation to your class about his or her work. Have the scientist explain how microbes have been used to make penicillin and clean up oil spills.

COMMON CORE
STATE STANDARDS

W.5.1–
W.5.10

Name_____ Date_____

Read the passages.

Save the School Music Program

1. Dear Editor,

2. The Fairmount Area School District recently announced that it is looking for ways to lower costs for the new school year. The school board suggested that it could save money by shutting down the music education program. I am shocked by this development. I believe the music education program is an important part of a student's learning experience. It should not be cut just to save a few dollars.

3. Ending music education would not benefit our students. In fact, it might actually harm them. Music is a unique class. It gives the students learning experiences that go beyond homework and tests.

4. Music offers students the chance to express themselves creatively in ways that cannot be accomplished in regular classes. It also provides an important outlet for students who are musically gifted.

5. The benefits of the music program are not limited to the music classroom. Music can be tied to other subjects as well. For example, exposure to different cultural backgrounds through music helps students understand world cultures. Learning how instruments work helps students develop a clearer picture of concepts such as sound waves and vibration.

6. I understand that the school district needs to lower its costs— but the best way to save money is to spend less on athletic programs. I know this may not be a popular idea. It is, however, the right one.

(continued)

Name_____ Date_____

COMMON CORE
STATE STANDARDS
W.5.1–
W.5.10

(continued)

7.   While the athletic program has its place in our schools, I think too much money is devoted to it. This program receives more money than any other program in our school district. It actually receives more funds than it needs to operate. Some of this extra money could be used to support other education programs, such as music.

8.   We should not allow the music education program to be lost over money. Education should always be put ahead of sports or other activities. The music education program is too important to lose. I urge the school board to consider other ways to save money that will not take music education away from our students.

9.   Sincerely,

10.   Paul Rosen

(continue to next passage)

COMMON CORE
STATE STANDARDS

W.5.1–
W.5.10

Name_____ Date_____

(continued)

Cut the School Music Program

1. Dear Editor,

2. I read in your newspaper that the Fairmount Area School District wants to save money by cutting the school music program. I think this is a great idea and a good move by the school board. Music is nice, but it is not an important school subject. We should not be spending money on it when we could use that money elsewhere.

3. Students do not need to learn about music in school. Our schools should focus more on important academic subjects. English, science, and math classes are much more vital to the long-term well-being of our students than music. The money that is currently spent on the music education program could be used to buy better textbooks and equipment to support these classes.

4. Isn't education about preparing young people for the real world? Music classes don't do much for students once they're out of school. However, academic subjects do. They provide kids with the skills they need to get a job or succeed in college. That's why we should focus on improving academic areas instead of worrying about music and art.

5. I have heard some people suggest that we should take money away from athletic programs to keep the music program alive. I think this is a bad idea! Sports are just as important to students as English, science, and math. Sports teach students about fitness and allow them to stay healthy. Sports also helps kids learn about the value of teamwork. Being on a sports team shows kids how to work together to achieve important goals.

6. Keeping the music program by spending less on athletics would also be bad for the larger school community. Our sports program helps other clubs raise money. Many school clubs rely on community recognition of our athletic teams because it helps them raise funds for activities. If we start giving school sports less support, these other programs will suffer, too.

7. I know some people like music, but the music program is just not as important as academic subjects and sports. We need to make sure that the programs that are most important to our students get the most attention and money. We should end the music education program so that we have more money to spend where it is needed.

8. Sincerely,

9. Edward Mitchell

Name_____ Date_____

COMMON CORE
STATE STANDARDS
**W.5.1–
W.5.10**

Opinion/Argument Prompt

**Which letter do you think is the most persuasive and why? Support
your opinion with reasons from both letters and your own ideas.**

Informative/Explanatory Prompt

**Compare and contrast how the authors of both letters feel about
the school's athletic program. Use details from both letters to
support your explanation.**

Narrative Prompt

**Choose the letter you most agree with and write a positive response
from the president of the school board. Use words such as *I* and *me*
and explain how you will support the letter writer's request.**

COMMON CORE
STATE STANDARDS
W.5.1–
W.5.10

Name_____ Date_____

Read the passage below.

The Mayfield Paint Company

New Office Recycling Plan

1.   Many used office items can be recycled instead of being thrown away. Offices with a smart recycling plan can reduce the amount of garbage they throw away. Most garbage ends up in landfills. By recycling, we can do our part to help the environment.

2.   Our company is starting a new recycling plan. To make our recycling plan a success, we have provided some instructions for employees. Follow these steps:

3.   1.   Before throwing anything away, ask yourself if it can be recycled. Common items like paper, cardboard, and plastics can be recycled. If you're not sure if an item is recyclable, check for a recycling symbol. This symbol means that an item can be recycled. If the item can't be recycled, throw it into the garbage. Food and metals can't be recycled.

4.   2.   Find the right recycling bin. We have set up several bins for the different types of items. For example, we have set up a bin for paper, another for cardboard, and a third for plastic items. The paper and cardboard bins are located next to the copy machine. The plastic bin is in the kitchen area.

5.   3.   Figure out if the item can fit into the bin. If the item is too big, do what it takes to make the item smaller. For example, you can fold paper or break down a cardboard box. Plastic items, however, might be tricky to fit into the bin. If the item is soft enough, place it on the floor and carefully stomp it with your foot. This should help the item to fit. If the plastic item is hard, do not stomp on it! Instead, put the item next to the bin. You might attach a note to show that the item should be recycled.

6.   4.   Place the item in the bin, and that's it! Our cleaning company will empty the bins twice each week.

7.   Thank you for following this policy. Our company uses many paper, cardboard, and plastic items. We hope this recycling program will help us do a better job in saving the environment.

(continue to next passage)

Common Core Writing to Texts Grade 5 • ©2014 Newmark Learning, LLC

Name_____ Date_____

(continued)

The Mayfield Paint Company

Saving Paper

1.   Wasted paper is not good for our office—or for Earth. Paper comes from trees. Using a lot of paper means many trees are cut down. If the paper is wasted, those trees have been cut down for nothing. Paper is also expensive. We should try to save money on paper when we can.

2.   Going forward, all employees should try to reduce their paper use. Follow these guidelines to get started.

3.   1.   Set up your printer so that it prints on both sides of the paper. This allows you to print two pages on one sheet of paper.

4.   2.   Always set the copy machine to copy double-sided, or on both sides of the paper.

5.   3.   Reuse printer paper when possible. You probably have a stack of printer paper that has been printed on one side of the sheet. Do not throw this stack away. Instead, load the paper into the printer with the blank side facing up. This allows you to print on the other side of the paper.

6.   4.   Reuse notepad paper whenever possible. If you usually only write on one side of the page, try using both. Some people turn their notebook around and start a "fresh" notebook using the back sides of the pages.

(continued)

COMMON CORE
STATE STANDARDS
W.5.1–
W.5.10

Name_____ Date_____

(continued)

7. 5. Before you print, ask yourself if you really need to print the document. Try editing and proofreading electronically so that you don't have to print a document more than once.

8. 6. Make sure you print only the pages you need. Don't print extra pages just because that's the easier printer option.

9. 7. Work with our customers so they will choose to receive documents electronically. This is faster and easier—and costs less in paper, ink, and postage.

10. 8. Don't print documents for storage. Keep an electronic version instead.

11. 9. Make sure you recycle all of your used paper.

12. Thank you for following this policy.

Name_____ Date_____

COMMON CORE
STATE STANDARDS
W.5.1–
W.5.10

Opinion/Argument Prompt

Do you think the employees of the Mayfield Paint Company will participate in the new recycling plan and follow the guidelines for reducing the amount of paper they use? Why or why not? Support your opinion with reasons from both texts.

Informative/Explanatory Prompt

Explain the company's new policy for recycling and reducing the amount of paper used. Support your explanation with details from both texts.

Narrative Prompt

Write a story in which a company employee tries to convince another employee to participate in the new recycling program and reduce the amount of paper he or she uses. Give the characters names, and include dialogue in your story.

COMMON CORE
STATE STANDARDS
W.5.1–
W.5.10

Name_____ Date_____

Read the passages.

The Times

THURSDAY, MAY 20, 1869

First Transcontinental Railroad Completed, May 10, 1869

1. After six long years of construction, the nation's first national railroad system has been completed. The rail line is known as the First Transcontinental Railroad. It connects the eastern and western halves of the United States. Soon travelers will be able to ride the rails from one end of the country clear to the other.

2. The Union Pacific and Central Pacific Railroad Companies celebrated their accomplishment with a ceremony in Utah. Here they joined the eastern and western halves of the tracks. Leland Stanford, president of Central Pacific, was given the honor of driving the final spike into the rails. The large crowd on hand laughed when Stanford's first swing completely missed its mark. His next few swings were more successful, and bells and whistles rang out with each tap of the spike.

3. The national railroad has a long history. Asa Whitney, an American businessman, first suggested the railroad in 1845. Members of Congress were interested in the idea. However, they could not give it much attention due to more pressing national issues. The railroad plan finally moved forward in 1861. That's when the Central Pacific Railroad Company was formed in California. This company, led by Theodore Judah and Collis P. Huntington, got the project off the ground.

4. To fund the project, Congress passed a special bill in 1862. The bill divided the work between the Central Pacific and another newly formed company, the Union Pacific Railroad. Central Pacific was charged with laying the tracks heading east from California. Union Pacific was charged with laying the tracks heading west from the Missouri River. Both companies employed large numbers of men. They faced long hours, harsh weather, difficult landscapes, and many other problems.

5. At first, the workers heading west worked more quickly. They were able to lay a long length of track. The men heading east were off to a slower start. Their territory included harsh mountain ranges. Eventually, this group began to move more quickly.

6. The two companies finally met in Utah. They joined the final lengths of track with a golden spike. By the time the two groups met, Union Pacific had laid 690 miles of the track. Central Pacific had laid 1,086 miles of the track.

(continue to next passage)

Name_____ Date_____

COMMON CORE
STATE STANDARDS
W.5.1–
W.5.10

(continued)

Westward Rails
by Jonah Whitley

1.   In April 1872, I convinced my wife, Emily, to join me on a trip across the United States on the great rail line that had been built to connect the East and West some years earlier.

2.   Emily wasn't terribly thrilled about the idea. She was convinced that it would be a long and uncomfortable journey. She was also worried by stories of train wrecks. Luckily, I was able to talk her into it.

3.   Our first surprise came when we bought our tickets in New York City. We learned that the trip to California would cost us only about $150! While that is a lot of money, before the new railroad, it would have cost us about $1,000.

4.   We were amazed as we boarded the train that would take us from New York to Nebraska. We had our very own sleeping compartment with a sofa that turned into a bed. It was larger than I imagined. Emily seemed quite pleased with our quarters.

5.   The train let out a great puff of smoke as it left the station. We soon learned that we would have to get used to a great deal of smoke and dust during our trip. I spoke to the conductor, and he told me that we would be traveling at speeds between 9 and 35 miles per hour. Incredible!

6.   We stopped at many stations along the way. We ate our meals at these stations because the train did not have a dining car. The food was good, but we had to eat many of the same things over and over. We had fried eggs, sweet potatoes, and buffalo steaks quite a few times. I don't think Emily liked that much.

(continued)

Common Core
State Standards

W.5.1–
W.5.10

Name_____ Date_____

(continued)

7.   Herds of wild buffalo became a common sight for us after we changed trains in Nebraska. They often surrounded our train in great numbers. Emily and I had never seen buffalo before. We were both amazed at the size of the great beasts.

8.   Crossing through the plains was an interesting experience. The grasses were shorter than we expected, but they moved with the wind like waves on the ocean. After a while, though, the unchanging scenery seemed a bit dull.

9.   That all changed when we reached the mountains. The beautiful ranges that led us into California were cold and snowy. We were struck with awe when we learned that we had reached a height of 7,017 feet.

10.   We finally headed back down the other side of the mountains and arrived in the sunny Sacramento Valley. Emily grasped my arm as we entered the station. She looked up at me with a smile and thanked me for taking her on such a wonderful journey.

Common Core Writing to Texts Grade 5 • ©2014 Newmark Learning, LLC

Name_____ Date_____

COMMON CORE
STATE STANDARDS
W.5.1–
W.5.10

Opinion/Argument Prompt

How do you think the Transcontinental Railroad changed people's lives? Support your opinion with details from both texts as well as your own ideas.

Informative/Explanatory Prompt

What can you tell about the mountains people encountered while they worked or traveled on the rail? Support your explanation with details from both texts.

Narrative Prompt

Write a story in which Jonah and Emily Whitley meet some of the men who built the Transcontinental Railroad. Using dialogue, have Jonah and Emily discuss their trip and thank the men for their hard work.

COMMON CORE
STATE STANDARDS

W.5.1–
W.5.10

Name_____ Date_____

Read the passages.

The Brooklyn Flea

1. American flea markets have charmed bargain shoppers for decades. Flea markets are large, open-air shopping spaces. Many different vendors gather together to offer shoppers a variety of goods. Shoppers look for all kinds of items, including manufactured wares, antiques, and handmade goods.

2. When flea markets first appeared in small-town America in the 1950s, they were generally small and didn't offer a big variety of items. However, they quickly became popular. People flocked to the markets in search of bargains. As a result, some flea markets expanded. A few started to cover several city blocks! Flea markets became common in small towns and large cities alike.

3. One of the most famous flea markets in America is the Brooklyn Flea in New York City. This market attracts thousands of visitors every week. The Brooklyn Flea opened its doors in 2008 and offers year-round shopping. The market is held outdoors when the weather is warm and indoors when the weather cools. The Brooklyn Flea offers up to 150 merchants. These merchants are versatile but have one thing in common: They are based in and around New York City. The merchants sell a wide variety of items, such as antiques, old clothing, furniture, jewelry, and handmade arts and crafts.

4. The Brooklyn Flea brings natives and tourists together to share in a fun-filled shopping experience. Shoppers don't even have to worry about meals. They can spend the whole day bargain hunting while dining at one of the many food vendors inside the market. The food vendors offer a variety of regional and foreign dishes. The food vendors are so popular that the Brooklyn Flea opened Smorgasburg, a food market, just for food shopping and dining!

5. The owners of the Brooklyn Flea eventually started to offer the market in different places around New York City. Savvy shoppers can now find the Brooklyn Flea near the Brooklyn Bridge as well as in Central Park. The Brooklyn Flea has received much praise for its contributions to New York City living. The market highlights local businesses and has earned a solid reputation among both city dwellers and business owners.

6. Places like the Brooklyn Flea can be found all over the world. Each market contains a unique mixture of local goods, both new and old. From California to Japan, people around the globe can find all sorts of interesting treasures at their local flea markets.

(continue to next passage)

Name_____ Date_____

(continued)

A Grand Bazaar in Turkey

1. Long before people sold goods at garage sales and flea markets, the country of Turkey offered the Grand Bazaar. The Grand Bazaar originated with a great Turkish sultan in ancient times.

2. The sultan wanted to show the world the many riches of his land. He built a grand hall in Turkey where people could buy and sell goods. He constructed two giant domed buildings in the great city of Istanbul.

3. These buildings allowed people to visit from all over the world. After it was built, the Grand Bazaar became an important trading base and operated for many centuries. In fact, it is still open today. Thousands of people visit the Grand Bazaar each day.

4. Merchants at the Grand Bazaar offer hand-painted pottery, hand-woven carpets, jewelry, local herbs and spices, and other fine goods. This historic trading center currently houses two houses of worship, four fountains, two Turkish baths, and many restaurants.

5. The bazaar takes up sixty streets in Istanbul and contains nearly 5,000 shops. The most valuable goods are offered in the bazaar's center. This area is known as the jewelry market. The natives call it the "hall of Cevahir Bedestan."

6. Precious gems and metals that are found only in Istanbul are bought and sold here. Beautiful jewelry made of coral and turquoise stones are offered alongside mother-of-pearl mirrors and amber beads. Other expensive items like antique furniture and old coins are also available.

(continued)

COMMON CORE
STATE STANDARDS
W.5.1–
W.5.10

Name_____ Date_____

(continued)

7.   People have been traveling to Turkey for hundreds of years to experience the colorful charms of the Grand Bazaar. Istanbul is known for its connections to important trading routes throughout the world.

8.   Visitors can experience the magic of the bazaar and wander the same streets that were once traveled by ancient tradespeople. The excitement of old Istanbul can be recalled by admiring the merchandise and bargaining over prices.

9.   The Grand Bazaar is one of the largest covered markets in the entire world. It has experienced several makeovers and even survived an earthquake. Thousands of stalls are filled with all kinds of specialty goods. It is almost impossible to leave without taking home a piece of the Grand Bazaar's treasure.

Name_____ Date_____

COMMON CORE
STATE STANDARDS
W.5.1–
W.5.10

 Opinion/Argument Prompt

Do you think a flea market is a good place to buy antiques? Why or why not? Support your opinion with details from both texts.

 Informative/Explanatory Prompt

Compare and contrast the Brooklyn Flea and the Grand Bazaar. Use details from both texts to support your explanation.

 Narrative Prompt

Write a story about someone who is visiting a large flea market for the first time. Use details from "The Brooklyn Flea" and "A Grand Bazaar in Turkey" to help you with your story.

Common Core
State Standards

W.5.1

W.5.4

W.5.5

Name_____ Date_____

Opinion/Argument Organizer

My Opinion:

Reason 1:	**Reason 2:**	**Reason 3:**
Supporting Details:	**Supporting Details:**	**Supporting Details:**

My Opinion Restated:

Name_____ Date_____

COMMON CORE
STATE STANDARDS
W.5.1
W.5.4
W.5.5

Name_____ Date_____

Opinion/Argument Organizer

Position Sentence:

Reason 1:	**Reason 2:**	**Reason 3:**
Reason 1 Evidence:	**Reason 2 Evidence:**	**Reason 3 Evidence:**

My Conclusion:

Name_____ Date_____

COMMON CORE
STATE STANDARDS

W.5.2

W.5.4

W.5.5

Name_____ Date_____

Informative/Explanatory Organizer

Topic:

Main Idea:

Evidence/Details:

COMMON CORE
STATE STANDARDS
W.5.2
W.5.4
W.5.5

Name_____ Date_____

Informative/Explanatory Organizer

Topic:

Main Point:	**Supporting Details:**
Main Point:	**Supporting Details:**
Main Point:	**Supporting Details:**

Name_____ Date_____

COMMON CORE
STATE STANDARDS

W.5.3

W.5.4

W.5.5

Name_____ Date_____

Narrative Organizer

Major Events

Name_____ Date_____

Name_____ Date_____

COMMON CORE
STATE STANDARDS
W.5.3
W.5.4
W.5.5

Narrative Organizer

Main Idea:

Details:

Name_____ Date_____

COMMON CORE
STATE STANDARDS

W.5.1–
W.5.5

Name_____ Date_____

✓ Writing Checklist: Opinion/Argument

- ❏ I introduced the topic.
- ❏ I stated a strong opinion, position, or point of view.
- ❏ I used well-organized reasons from both passages to support my opinion.
- ❏ I supported my reasons with facts and details.
- ❏ I used linking words and phrases to connect my opinion and reasons, such as *for instance*, *in order to*, and *in addition*.
- ❏ I ended with a conclusion that sums up and supports my position.
- ❏ I used correct grammar.
- ❏ I used correct capitalization, punctuation, and spelling.

✓ Writing Checklist: Informative/Explanatory

- ❏ I started with a clear topic statement.
- ❏ I grouped related information in paragraphs.
- ❏ I developed my topic with facts, definitions, concrete details, quotations, or other information and examples from the text.
- ❏ I linked ideas and information effectively using words, phrases, and clauses.
- ❏ I used precise language and terminology to explain the topic.
- ❏ I wrote a conclusion related to the information I presented.
- ❏ I reviewed my writing for good grammar.
- ❏ I reviewed my writing for capitalization, punctuation, and spelling.

Name_____ Date_____

COMMON CORE
STATE STANDARDS
**W.5.1–
W.5.5**

✔ Writing Checklist: Narrative

- ❏ I established a setting or situation for my narrative.
- ❏ I introduced a narrator and/or characters.
- ❏ I organized my narrative into a sequence of unfolding events.
- ❏ I used dialogue and description to develop events and show how characters respond to them.
- ❏ I used transitional words to show my sequence of events.
- ❏ I used concrete words and phrases and sensory details to describe events.
- ❏ I wrote a conclusion to the events in my narrative.
- ❏ I reviewed my writing for good grammar.
- ❏ I reviewed my writing for capitalization, punctuation, and spelling.

Rubrics and Assessments

Using the Rubrics to Assess Students and Differentiate Instruction

Use the Evaluation Rubrics on the next page to guide your assessment of students' responses. The rubrics are based on the Common Core State Standards for writing. Similar rubrics will be used by evaluators to score new standardized assessments.

After scoring students' writing, refer to the differentiated rubrics on pages 130–135. These are designed to help you differentiate your interactions and instruction to match students' needs. For each score a student receives in the Evaluation Rubrics, responsive prompts are provided to support writers. These gradual-release prompts scaffold writers toward mastery of each writing type.

• For a score of 1, use the Goal-Oriented prompts.

• For a score of 2, use the Directive and Corrective Feedback prompts.

• For a score of 3, use the Self-Monitoring and Reflection prompts.

• For a score of 4, use the Validating and Confirming prompts.

Using Technology

If you choose to have students use computers to write and revise their work, consider these ways to support online collaboration and digital publishing:

• Google Drive facilitates collaboration and allows teachers and peers to provide real-time feedback on writing pieces.

• Wikis enable students to share their writing around a common topic.

• Audio tools enable students to record their works (podcasts) for others to hear on a safe sharing platform.

• Student writing can be enriched with images, audio, and video.

Evaluation Rubrics

Student _____ Grade _____

Teacher _____ Date _____

Opinion/Argument				
Traits	**1**	**2**	**3**	**4**
The writer introduces the piece by stating a strong opinion.				
The writer supports the opinion with well-organized reasons and evidence.				
The writer uses words, phrases, and clauses to clarify the relationships among claim(s) and reasons.				
The writer provides a concluding statement or section that supports the position.				
The writer establishes and maintains a formal style.				
The writer demonstrates command of grade-appropriate conventions of standard English.				

Informative/Explanatory				
Traits	**1**	**2**	**3**	**4**
The writer includes a strong introduction.				
The writer organized ideas, concepts, and information logically.				
The writer uses relevant facts, definitions, concrete details, quotations, or other information and examples to develop his or her points.				
The writer uses appropriate transitions to connect ideas within categories of information.				
The writer provides a concluding statement or section that follows from the information presented.				
The writer demonstrates command of grade-appropriate conventions of standard English.				

Narrative				
Traits	**1**	**2**	**3**	**4**
The writer establishes a context and introduces a narrator and/or characters and organizes an event sequence that unfolds naturally.				
The writer uses narrative techniques, such as dialogue, pacing, and description to develop experiences and events or to show the responses of characters to situations.				
The writer uses a variety of transition words, phrases, and clauses to manage the sequence of events.				
The writer uses concrete words and phrases and details to convey experiences and events precisely.				
The writer provides a conclusion that follows from the narrated experiences or events.				
The writer demonstrates command of grade-appropriate conventions of standard English.				

Key

1–Beginning	2–Developing	3–Accomplished	4–Exemplary

Opinion/Argument

TRAITS	1: Goal-Oriented
The writer introduces the piece by stating a strong opinion.	When I start an opinion piece, I state my opinion or point of view. I need to tell exactly what my view is. After reading this prompt, I can state my opinion as ____.
The writer supports the opinion with well-organized reasons and evidence.	I need to think of two or three good reasons to support my opinion. My opinion about this prompt is ____. I'll jot down the evidence I need to support my opinion. Then I'll go back to my writing and include them.
The writer uses words, phrases, and clauses to clarify the relationships among claim(s) and reasons.	I need to link my reasons together using words and phrases, such as *consequently* and *specifically*. I am going to look for places where I can add these words and phrases.
The writer provides a concluding statement or section that supports the opinion.	When I finish writing an argument, I need to finish with a strong statement that supports my whole argument. When I conclude this argument, I can restate my opinion as ____.
The writer establishes and maintains a formal style.	When I write an opinion/argument, I want to sound confident and official when I make a claim. I will do this by using a formal and serious tone.
The writer demonstrates command of grade-appropriate conventions of standard English.	I am going to read through my writing to make sure that my pronouns are in the proper case. I will read through my whole argument to make sure that I have spelled words correctly.

2: Directive and Corrective Feedback	3: Self-Monitoring and Reflection	4: Validating and Confirming
Reread the first sentences of your writing. Then go back and reread the prompt. Did you clearly state an opinion that answers the prompt? Revise your statement to make it clear and focused.	Tell me how you chose _____ as your opinion. How can you make your position clearer for the reader?	I can see that your position is _____. You made your opinion very clear. That got me to pay attention to the issue.
What are your reasons for your opinion? Find supporting details and evidence in the text for each reason. Group these ideas together in separate paragraphs.	How did you decide to organize your ideas? Did you identify the information that was most relevant to your opinion? How did you do this?	You included some strong, relevant evidence to support your opinion.
I notice that you have more than one reason to support your opinion. What words can you add to show the reader that you are moving from one reason to another?	Show me a part of your argument where you link ideas using words and phrases. Show me a part where you could improve your writing by using linking words or phrases.	The words and phrases _____ and _____ are very effective at linking together the connection between your opinions and reasons. They help me understand your ideas.
Reread the last sentences of your argument. Does it end by restating your point of view? Go back and look at your opinion. How can you reinforce this idea in your conclusion?	How does your conclusion support your opinion or the position that you have taken? Is there a way you could make this conclusion stronger?	Your concluding section clearly supports your point of view. You've really convinced me that your opinion makes sense.
Let's read this paragraph again. Are there words that do not sound like words you would use in a formal setting? Let's change them to sound more formal.	Tell me what you did to make your style sound formal.	I notice how you sounded like an authority on the topic. I liked how your tone was serious.
Read that sentence again. Does it sound right to you? Your pronoun is ambiguous. How should you edit that?	Show me a place in your writing where you used commas correctly. What rule of punctuation did you apply?	Your argument included many varied sentences which you punctuated correctly.

Informative/Explanatory

TRAITS	1: Goal-Oriented
The writer includes a strong introduction.	When I start an informational/explanatory text, I introduce my topic. I'm going to think about what I want my readers to know about ____. Then I create a main idea statement.
The writer organized ideas, concepts, and information logically.	It is important that I group ideas together in an order that makes sense. I am going to categorize my information to help me structure the parts of my informative/explanatory text.
The writer uses relevant facts, definitions, concrete details, quotations, or other information and examples to develop his or her points.	I need to find facts and details from the text to support my points. I can go back to the text and underline parts that I think will help my writing. Then I will include them in my informative/ explanatory text.
The writer uses appropriate transitions to connect ideas within categories of information.	I need to connect my ideas together using linking words, such as *in contrast* and *especially*. I am going to look for places where I can add these words and phrases.
The writer provides a concluding statement or section that follows from the information presented.	When I finish writing an informative/explanatory text, I need to summarize my ideas in a conclusion. When I conclude, I can look back at my main idea statement, then restate it as ____.
The writer demonstrates command of grade-appropriate conventions of standard English.	I will make sure I have used quotation marks correctly when I've quoted directly from the text.

2: Directive and Corrective Feedback	3: Self-Monitoring and Reflection	4: Validating and Confirming
How could you introduce your topic in a way that tells exactly what you will be writing about?	Take a look at your main idea statement. Do you feel that it clearly introduces your topic?	Your main idea statement is clearly ____. That introduction helped me understand exactly what I was going to read about.
Put your facts and details into categories. These categories can be the sections of your informative/explanatory text.	How did you decide to organize your ideas? Did you look at an organizing chart? How did it help you?	You organized your informative/explanatory text into [number] well-defined sections.
What are your main points? Find supporting details and evidence in the text for each point.	Have you included all of the facts you wanted to share about ____.	You included some strong facts, definitions, and details to support your topic.
Let's read this paragraph. I see two related ideas. How can you link these ideas together?	Show me a part of your informative/explanatory text where you could improve your writing by using transitions.	The words and phrases ____ and ____ are very effective at linking together ideas.
Reread the last sentences of your informative/explanatory text. Do they restate your main idea?	Show me your concluding statement. Is there a way you could make this conclusion stronger?	After I read your conclusion, I felt I had really learned something from your writing.
Read that sentence again. Does it sound right to you? Some parts of your sentence do not agree. How should you edit that?	Show me a place where you made a correction. What was wrong and how did you fix it?	Your informative/explanatory text included many varied, complex sentences.

Narrative

TRAITS	1: Goal-Oriented
The writer establishes a context and introduces a narrator and/or characters and organizes an event sequence that unfolds naturally.	I will use a sequence of events chart to jot down the events I will write about. I will record details from the text I have already read. I will include those details in my new narrative.
The writer uses narrative techniques, such as dialogue, pacing, and description to develop experiences and events or to show the responses of characters to situations.	I want to include descriptions in my narrative. I will write down precise words that will help my readers picture what I am writing about. Then I will include these in my narrative.
The writer uses a variety of transition words, phrases, and clauses to manage the sequence of events.	When I write a narrative, I need to use signal words so that my reader does not get confused. I will add words and phrases such as *first, then, the next day,* and *later that week* to help my reader understand the order of events.
The writer uses concrete words and phrases and details to convey experiences and events precisely.	I will reread to look for words I have overused, Varying my word choice and making my words and phrases more precise will make my narrative more interesting to my readers.
The writer provides a conclusion that follows from the narrated experiences or events.	I am going to reread the ending of my narrative to make sure that it gives the reader a feeling of closure. I need to concentrate on how the problem in the narrative is solved.
The writer demonstrates command of grade-appropriate conventions of standard English.	I am going to read through my narrative to make sure that I formed and used both regular and irregular verbs correctly.

Common Core Writing to Texts Grade 5 • ©2014 Newmark Learning, LLC

2: Directive and Corrective Feedback	3: Self-Monitoring and Reflection	4: Validating and Confirming
Think of events that will lead from the problem to the resolution. You've decided to write about ____. Now think of the sequence of events you will include.	What graphic organizer could help you organize your narrative events? Tell me how you went about organizing your narrative.	The events you organized lead to a [fun, surprising, etc.] resolution.
Imagine that you're a character. What's happening in the narrative? What do you have to say to other characters? What do you have to say about the events?	How could you give each character a different voice in the dialogue?	I can visualize where your narrative takes place. You've included some nice descriptive details.
Let's read this paragraph. Is it clear to the reader when all the action is taking place? What words could you add to help the reader's understanding?	Show me where you used sequence signal words in your narrative. Show me a place where you could use signal words to make the order of events clearer.	The phrase ____ gave a nice transition between ____ and ____.
Notice the [action words, descriptive words] in your narrative. How could you make them stronger?	Show me where you revised some words to make the [experiences, events] clearer. How did your revision help?	I notice that you used [the idiom, description, figurative language, etc] to develop the character's dialogue. That really helped me hear the character's voice.
Let's read the ending of your narrative. Does it show how the problem is solved? Is there something you can add to make sure the reader feels as if the narrative piece is over?	Show me how your ending gives the reader a feeling of closure. Are there any questions from the narrative that you feel were unanswered?	You've developed an interesting resolution to the problem in your narrative. It gives me a sense of closure.
I got confused about the sequence when ____. Take another look at your verb tenses. Make sure they are consistent.	Show me a place in your writing where your sentences could be better. What could you do to improve them?	Your narrative included a lot of dialogue, and you used punctuation correctly.

Editing/Proofreading Symbols

Mark	What It Means	How to Use It
ℓ	Delete. Take something out here.	We went to to the store.
∧	Change or insert letter or word.	San Francico, Calafornia my home.
#	Add a space here.	My familyloves to watch baseball.
◯	Remove space.	We saw the sail boat streak by.
ℓ	Delete and close the space.	I gave the man my monney.
¶	Begin a new paragraph here.	"How are you?" I asked. "Great," said Jack.
↝	No new paragraph. Keep sentences together.	The other team arrived at one. The game started at once.
∼	Transpose (switch) the letters or words.	Thier friends came with gifts.
≡	Make this a capital letter.	mrs. smith
/	Make this a lowercase letter.	My Sister went to the City.
◯	Spell it out.	Mr. García has 3 cats.
⊙	Insert a period.	We ran home There was no time to spare
∧	Insert a comma.	We flew to Washington D.C.
∨	Insert an apostrophe.	Matts hat looks just like Johns.
⌄⌄	Insert quotation marks.	Hurry! said Brett.
?	Is this correct? Check it.	The Civil War ended in 1875.
STET	Ignore the edits. Leave as is.	Her hair was brown. STET